THE HILL

An Urban Political Thriller Screenplay

Christopher C. Odom

CreateSpace

Scotts Valley, CA

In cooperation with

Odom Books

Nashville, TN

Published by
CreateSpace
100 Enterprise Way, Suite A200, Scotts Valley, CA   95066

In cooperation with
Odom Books
135 Sundown Drive, Nashville, TN 37013

EAN-13: 9781438200651 (paperback)
ISBN-10: 143820065X (paperback) 1. Performing Arts / Screenplays

This is an Odom Books book.

THE HILL

An Original Screenplay By

Christopher C. Odom

FADE IN:

INT. CABIN - NIGHT

A passionate ORCHESTRAL SCORE (THE HILL MAIN THEME) plays on a variation of the ROOTS THEME.

One by one, SKETCHES are torn out of aged BOOKS and tossed into a FLAMING FIREPLACE. As each sketch is completely burned, another sketch is torn from a book and tossed into the fireplace.

SERIES OF SKETCHES

Adam and Eve are banished from the Garden of Eden.

The Tower of Babel is destroyed in Babylon.

Imhotep constructs the first pyramid for the Pharaoh Zoser.

The Pharaoh's daughter takes in baby Moses.

Greek philosophers study at the Library of Carthage.

Jesus is crucified on the cross.

The Pope hangs a painting of Black Madonna in his office.

Olmec Heads are constructed in South America.

The Moors invade Spain.

The Moorish Empire falls during the crusades.

Slaves are shipped to America on the "Good Ship Jesus."

Afrika is colonized.

                                        CUT TO BLACK:

BLACK SCREEN

Pages are torn from a calendar which dial back the year. The years dial back from A.D. to B.C. until there is nothing left but darkness. These words appear where the calendar was:

                    IN THE BEGINNING...

                                        CUT TO:

BLACK SCREEN

There are three carved holes at the bottom of the screen: triangle, circle, square. A challenged HAND forces a SQUARE PEG into a round hole. Once the hand is removed from the square peg, it reveals the word:

<u>**ORIENTATION**</u>

CUT TO:

INT. BOXING RING - NIGHT

All of the KEY PLAYERS IN THE MOVIE - whom you're yet to meet - are spread out across the screen, eyes directed forward: the Pre-Alumni Association members in power suits, the Chapel Assistants in clergy collars, and the Disciples of ANKH in Afrikan robes. The Pre-Alumni Members, the Chapel Assistants, and Disciples of ANKH all wear BOXING GLOVES.

The floor of the boxing ring is covered with a FLAT MAP OF THE WORLD.

Meet ADAM (17), he's all that's American - baseball, Cracker Jacks, and apple pie. Adam wears a GOLD PINKY RING on his right-hand engraved with the initials "A.L.E." beneath a small DIAMOND.

Adam stands in the center of the screen. He wears a LETTERMAN SWEATER, which reads: "THE HILL." He stares directly at the camera.

Now, say hello to CHANCELLOR DIX (58). He's light skinned and full of pretentious honor and overplayed grandeur.

Chancellor Dix sits at the judges' table garbed in a GENERAL'S MILITARY DRESS.

Adjacent to Chancellor Dix, garbed in a complimenting ADMIRAL'S MILITARY DRESS, is DEAN RICHARDS (52). He would be better placed as a Baptist Television evangelist instead of aging in academia.

LIESL, dressed as a ring card girl, walks into the center of the ring and holds up a RING CARD which reads:

(EVERY MAN 4 HIMSELF)

Adam smacks the gloves of the two students closest to him. As all the students bump gloves together with a fighter form an opposing camp, a BELL RINGS.

CUT TO:

EXT. GYMNASIUM - NIGHT

College age Afrikan-American men squeeze through the doors of a rustic gym. The MARQUEE reads:

1991-1992 Hillfield University Freshman Orientation Week

                    ADAM (V.O.)
          August 28th, 1990. Freshmen Week at
          Hillfield University, or "The Hill" as
          they like to call it. It's where boyhood
          ends and manhood begins. The Hill is a
          microcosm of the real world. What you
          experience here, you will experience in
          the world, but tenfold.

INT. GYMNASIUM - NIGHT

All of the freshmen sit on the floor of the gym.

Adam crouches next to T.J. and WINSTON. T.J. (18), dark skinned, is a pure blood bumpkin equipped with a homemade Jheri curl. Winston (17), light skinned, could be the spokesperson for "Snobs-R-Us".

TWELVE UPPERCLASSMEN DISCIPLES OF ANKH stand at attention underneath a basketball hoop in a straight line. They are all dark-skinned Afrikan-Americans. Each Disciple wears matching combat boots in addition to an array of traditional style "Back to Afrika" garb - robes, beads, and ankh necklaces. Each Disciple's head is evenly partitioned with sprouting dreadlock twists.

At the end of the row of Twelve Disciples stands a thirteenth Disciple, KAREEM (21), Assistant Ra of ANKH. He wears a different robe and his locks are long and flowing.

OSIRIS parades amidst the freshmen in a baggy cotton traditional Afrikan gown while he clutches a STAFF forged of hardened root. Osiris (22), is a light skinned, green eyed Afrikan-American man with a deep resounding commanding voice, long flowing locks, and lengthy bushy beard.

                    OSIRIS
          My brothers, there are...
              (raises staff)
          Three things...

The Disciples snap to parade-rest and each present THREE FINGERS.

                         DISCIPLES
          Three!

                       OSIRIS (CONT'D)
          That I must leave you with before you
          go tonight.

Osiris lowers his STAFF.

The Disciples return to attention.

                          OSIRIS
          Number One. Be on time! A Hillfield
          Man is always on time. To be on time,
          means to be fifteen minutes early.

          While you rush to get to work, in just
          enough time, to be late as <u>hell</u>, the
          white devils have been there for three
          hours.

          They've read the paper, had breakfast
          together, and talked about you. Be on
          time!

The freshmen CHUCKLE.

                           T.J.
                  (during the silence)
          Oh lawd, who the fuck is this guy?

                          OSIRIS
                       (shouts)
          Who am I?

Osiris POUNDS HIS STAFF TWICE on the floor.

Kareem marches out of formation next to Osiris.

                          KAREEM
          Sir, your name is Osiris, sir!
                        (roars)
          Ra, of ANKH, sir!

Kareem marches back into formation and snaps to attention.

The freshmen LAUGH.

                           T.J.
          Ra?

The Hill

                         WINSTON
          It's equivalent to basileus, but in
          lieu of being a Greek Frat, it's
          Afrikan.

                         T.J.
          Basileus?

                         OSIRIS
          Number Two.

Raises STAFF.

The Disciples snap to parade rest and each present TWO FINGERS.

                         DISCIPLES
          Two!

                         ADAM
                    (to T.J.)
          Shhh. He's moving on to number two.

Winston and T.J. look at Adam, and both ROLL THEIR EYES.

                         OSIRIS (CONT'D)
          A Hillfield Man always has a pen.

Osiris removes a PEN from his gown.

The Disciples snap to attention. They flex INK PENS.

                         FRESHMEN VOICE
          That's to write down the numbers of our
          Springfield Sisters.

                         OSIRIS
          The key to a good memory is writing it
          down. You can always tell a Hillfield
          Man. But, you can never tell him much.

LAUGHS.

A few of the freshmen wave PENS.

                         OSIRIS
          And my brothers, **Number Three.**

The Disciples snap to attention.

                              DISCIPLES
                    Three!

Osiris stands next to T.J.

                               OSIRIS
                    A Hillfield Man, never, never, <u>ever</u>,
                    has a Jheri curl.

PANDEMONIUM.

The freshmen lift T.J. up above their heads. They bounce him around
like a beach ball.

                              DISCIPLES
                    The Hill!

It's catchy. Freshmen repeat it at random.

Osiris POUNDS HIS STAFF TWICE on the gymnasium floor and
outstretches his arms, gown draping, like Moses at the Red Sea.

The Disciples march in place.

Kareem leads the marching disciples through the sea of freshmen.

                               KAREEM
                         (chants)
                    RAIN...

                              DISCIPLES
                         (chants)
                    CAN'T STOP THE HILL!

                               KAREEM
                    SLEET...

                              DISCIPLES
                         (chants)
                    CAN'T STOP THE HILL!

                               KAREEM
                         (chants, imitating a
                         girl)
                    SPRINGFIELD...

                              DISCIPLES
                         (chants)
                    MAY SHOCK THE HILL!

                         ALL
                       (chants)
                BUT, NO ONE STOPS THE HILL!

Freshmen quickly pick up the tune and all CHANT in unison ad nauseam.

Osiris boldly points his staff at HOSEA JOHNSON (23), Chancellor
of the Chapel Assistants. A clergy collar hugs Hosea's throat and
a SCOFIELD BIBLE bound in a LEATHER CASE is perched under his arm.
Hosea is accompanied by SEVEN CHAPEL ASSISTANTS each with matching
collars and LEATHER BIBLE CASES.

Among the Chapel Assistants are MORGAN and EVERS. Morgan (20), would
be better named as "Malcolm Machiavelli." Evers (22), Vice
Chancellor of the Chapel Assistants, is a portly, jolly fellow who
is far too nice to completely trust.

Hosea coldly locks EYES with Osiris.

Hosea removes a CIGAR from his coat pocket. He holds it erect, for
a beat, next to his head, then bites the tip off, and spits it out
in Osiris' direction.

                                          TIME CUT TO:

INT. GYMNASIUM - NIGHT

T.J. attempts to cross Osiris' path in order to talk to some of the
fellas, but is met with the strong arming PALM of DISCIPLE JONAS
(21), an over zealous follower.

                    DISCIPLE JONAS
                Stand back, my brother. Osiris is
                coming through.

Osiris tunnels between two rows of marching ANKH Disciples. His gown
flows behind him like the train of an Emperor returning home from
a long day's conquest. Disciple Jonas leans over and whispers into
Osiris' ear.

                    DISCIPLE JONAS
                You will be the next Hillfield
                University Student Government
                President.

Kareem steps out of line and puts his arm around T.J.

                         KAREEM
                      (whispers)
          I used to have a Jheri curl, too. You
          can look a brother up if you want. I'm
          the R.A. on the first floor of Anderson
          Hall.

Winks.

                                              CUT TO:

EXT. CHAPEL - NIGHT

A lone STATUE of Frederick E. Hillfield towers in front of the barren
walk of an ominous chapel.

INT. CHAPEL - STAGE - NIGHT

Hosea stands on a DIMLY LIT stage encapsulated by a VINTAGE PIPE
ORGAN. Hosea is positioned in front of a podium upon which rests
his Scofield Bible encapsulated in a soft leather case. The Chapel
Assistants stand by close in a row of solidarity. Morgan is on
Hosea's right-hand side and Evers is on Hosea's left-hand side.

                         HOSEA
          In the words and the wisdom of the old
          Chinese proverb, it is better to light
          a lantern in the night than it is to
          curse the darkness.

The house lights go down. A SILHOUETTED FIGURE OF REV. MARTIN LUTHER
KING, JR. raises and LIGHTS A LANTERN. His back is to the audience.

[EXCERPT FROM THE REV. MARTIN LUTHER KING, JR.'S "I HAVE A DREAM
SPEECH" DELIVERED ON THE STEPS OF THE LINCOLN MEMORIAL IN
WASHINGTON D.C. ON AUGUST 28, 1963]

MALE CHORALERS, dressed in all black, slowly walk up the aisles from
the front of the chapel towards the back of the chapel. Each choraler
carries a single LANTERN, which illuminates his own face. They sing
the WENDELL P. WHALUM ARRANGEMENT OF "LIFT EVERY VOICE AND SING (THE
NEGRO NATIONAL ANTHEM)."

KING SILHOUETTE	MALE CHORUS
	(SINGS)
I have a dream,	
	LIFT EVERY VOICE
That one day this nation will	
rise up and live out the true	AND SING
meaning of its creed: "We hold	
these truths to be self-evident:	TILL EARTH AND
that all men are created	
equal."...	HEAVEN RING,
	RING WITH THE HARMONIES...

                          MALE CHORUS
                             (SINGS)
                       LIFT EVERY VOICE
                       AND SING
                       TILL EARTH AND
                       HEAVEN RING,
                       RING WITH THE HARMONIES...

INT. CHAPEL - SEATS - NIGHT

Winston YAWNS.

                          WINSTON
                 I'm going to the block party.

Winston leaves.

                          T.J.
                          (to Adam)
                 Coming?

                          ADAM
                 I'll catch up with you guys later.

INT. CHAPEL - STAGE - NIGHT

The Chapel Assistants join arms with Hosea, Morgan, and Evers.

The King Silhouette BLOWS OUT his LANTERN.

                                                       CUT TO:

INT. CHAPEL - BACKSTAGE - NIGHT

JOHN MASON makes eye contact from the wing with Hosea who is still
on stage. Hosea raises a LANTERN to his face and smiles.

John Mason (22), is the self-proclaimed despot and Premiere of the Pre-Alumni Association.

John is accompanied by five officers from the Pre-Alumni Association. They all wear power costumes: blue suits, white shirts, and red ties. Among the officers are TERRELL and LAWRENCE.

Terrell (21), Associate Premiere of the Pre-Alumni Association, is a dark skinned cavalier born leader.

Lawrence (21), is a wryly passive aggressive with the weight of the world in his electromagnetic glasses.

John whips out a CIGAR and LIGHTS it. Without breaking eye contact, he flicks ASHES onto the stage, then walks away.

                                        TIME CUT TO:

INT. CHAPEL - NIGHT

It's post performance hour. Hosea is well guarded by his posse of preachers - the Chapel Assistants.

RONALD ROLLINS (30), slick and clean-cut, the Resident Director of Packard Hall, warmly wraps one arm around Hosea and clasps Hosea's hand with the other. Ronald wears a CLERGY COLLAR.

Hosea inconspicuously slides an ENVELOP into Ronald's hand.

                    RONALD
          Looks like you might be the next
          Hillfield University Student
          Government President.

                    HOSEA
          No doubt.

As Hosea and Ronald separate hands, Ronald slips the envelop into his pocket.

                    RONALD
              (winks)
          Be sure to give me the list for your
          floor in the morning.

                    HOSEA
              (winks back)
          Already done.

Ronald disappears into the crowd.

The Hill

Adam scurries to the front of the stage to greet Hosea.

                    ADAM
          Hosea, I thought your message was-

Adam is sideswiped by Morgan.

                    MORGAN
          Hosea needs time for prayer.

Morgan turns his back to Adam. Morgan covers Hosea, drenched with
SWEAT, with a CAPE. Hosea, Morgan, and the Chapel Assistants walk
away. Evers grabs Adam by the HAND. Firmly shakes it.

                    EVERS
          Come to Chapel. Or if you just want to
          kick it, I'm the R.A. on the second
          floor of Packard Hall.

                                        CUT TO:

EXT. STREET CORNER - NIGHT

Several men from The Hill and sisters from Springfield congregate
on the street corner. They sip on ORANGE JUICE and VODKA from PLASTIC
CUPS. Several sisters wear tight BIKER SHORTS revealing every nook
and cranny while other sisters let it all hang out from DAISY DUKES
and BIKINI TOPS. A BUFF DRUNK BROTHER with no shirt on SPRAYS a
scantily clad sister with CHAMPAGNE. Wet T-shirt time.

A NIGERIAN MERCHANT has set up a table where he's peddling INCENSE,
HAND BAGS, SCENTED OILS, HANDMADE JEWELRY, AND BOOTLEG COMPACT
DISCS.

Adam approaches Winston and T.J. who are in the midst of a
conversation with two Springfield Sisters: LIESL (18), and KANEISHA
JACKSON-WASHINGTON (18). Liesl and Kaneisha lean against a
CONVERTIBLE JAGUAR XJS. Kaneisha is an around-the-way girl trying
to make good, while Liesl is everything that Adam desires and
doesn't possess.

T.J., topsy-turvy and quite tipsy, slings his arm around Adam and
sloshes screwdriver on Winston's shirt.

                    T.J.
          Bro', this is Liesl and Kaneisha. They
          go to Springfield.

Winston ROLLS HIS EYES at T.J. and fans the stench of T.J.'s breath.

12.

Adam touches Liesl's hand. Smiles. There is chemistry.

EVERS watches Adam from afar.

CLAUDE DUBOSE (25), a high-yellow, wavy-haired, fifth year senior, steps in front of Winston, T.J., and Adam. Claude whips out a KEY CHAIN and BEEPS an ALARM on the Jag.

>   CLAUDE DUBOSE
>   (to the girls)
>   I'm making a liquor run. Wanna' roll?

Liesl and Kaneisha giggle with approval.

>   CUT TO:

INT. ADAM'S DORM ROOM - NIGHT

An ALARM CLOCK reads: "4:00 A.M."

EXT. THE QUAD - NIGHT

Four buildings face each other from four corners of a vast grassy court. Three are dormitories and one is the Administration Building (Hillfield Hall).

John Mason stands in the center of the Quad while Terrell stands on his right-hand side and Lawrence stands on his left hand side.

John dons an indulgent OVERCOAT with baggy shoulders and a tale that just misses touching the ground. It's complimented by a coordinated paisley SILK SCARF, ASCOT, and pair of sleek LEATHER GLOVES clasp in his hands.

John raises his right hand for a beat, then lets it fall to his side.

>   SLAM CUT TO:

INT. ADAM'S DORMITORY - NIGHT

Adam, Winston, and T.J. rest nestled in their individual beds of a comfy triplex dorm room until they are rudely awakened by the sound of a FIRE ALARM BUZZ. A Pre-Alumni Association member (PETE) BURSTS into the room.

>   PRE-ALUMNI PETE
>   Get your ass up, niggaz! There's a
>   fire!

The Hill

Adam, Winston, and T.J. leap out of bed. Adam tries to put on his pants. T.J. doesn't move. Winston reaches for his robe.

Pete pushes T.J. out of the bed. He falls on the floor and moans.

                    T.J.
          Not now honey, I have a headache.

Adam helps T.J. stand.

                    PETE
          Move!!!

                                        CUT TO:

EXT. STREET - NIGHT

One thousand Afrikan-American Hillfield freshmen jog down a street in the heart of the ghetto. Some are in PAJAMAS, some are in HOUSE SHOES, and some are in UNDERWEAR. Others don't have on shirts, others are run while half asleep, and others are confused and frightened. Adam, Winston, and T.J. are among them. T.J. is miserably hung over.

Several Pre-Alumni Association Members in OVERLY STARCHED MATCHING JOGGING SUITS lead the pack.

The impoverished PEOPLE FROM THE PROJECTS line the streets as spectators.

Several AFRIKAN-AMERICAN POLICE keep the crowd safely on the sidewalk behind POLICE BARRICADES.

INT. EXOTIC CONVERTIBLE - NIGHT

John Mason schleps along in the back seat of an exotic convertible. Terrell faithfully serves as John Mason's driver and Lawrence John Mason's valet.

EXT. STREET - NIGHT

HOMELESS HENRY (44), eyes John Mason.

Homeless Henry slips underneath a BARRICADE and starts jogging with the students. He waves to crowd. Henry catches up with the convertible and touches John Mason on the shoulder.

                    HOMELESS HENRY
          Say, brother man, how about some spare
          change?

INT. EXOTIC CONVERTIBLE - NIGHT

John Mason indignantly frowns at Homeless Henry. POLICE OFFICER
BLACK tackles Homeless Henry and drags him away from the
convertible.

                    HOMELESS HENRY
         Fuck y'all Hill Niggaz, then.

EXT. STREET - NIGHT

T.J. ceases to run.

                    T.J.
                (to Adam)
        Ah, shit. I'm about to hurl.

T.J. turns and hurls his breakfast, lunch, and dinner in John
Mason's direction.

INT. EXOTIC CONVERTIBLE - NIGHT

Lawrence whips out a HANDKERCHIEF, and quickly brushes off the spot
on John Mason's overcoat that Homeless Henry touched.

                                  THEN:

Mini chunks of T.J.'s upchuck land on John Mason's coat in the same
spot where Lawrence wiped.

EXT. STREET - NIGHT

Adam puts his arm around T.J.

                    ADAM
        Can't stop now. Keep going. You can do
        it.

                                  CUT TO:

EXT. GRAVEYARD - NIGHT

The freshmen, soiled and sweaty, pant as John Mason glides on foot
between them. Terrell and Lawrence trail close behind.

John Mason interrupts his gait when he arrives at a MAUSOLEUM. He
stares at the sky for a beat, then turns to face the freshmen.

                    JOHN MASON
          The tomb of our founder-the Rev. Dr.
          Frederick E. Hillfield.
                    (beat)
          As far back as my family lineage lays,
          the men in my family have always been
          Hillfield Men and the women Springfield
          Women.

Winston nods affirmatively.

                    JOHN MASON
          Hillfield University has a long, proud,
          rich history of tradition. And I will
          not allow myself or anyone else to
          dishonor my Hillfield family's name.

A single TEAR crawls down John Mason's cheek.

                    JOHN MASON
          You will not bring dishonor upon this
          Hill.

John Mason reaches down on the ground and picks up a CROWN. As he
raises the crown above his head, the SUN RISES above the Tomb of
Frederick E. Hillfield, and shines rays of light through the center
of the crown.

                    JOHN MASON
          Hillfield University places a crown
          above all of our heads, and it's up to
          each and every one of us to aspire to
          it.

Winston is moved.

                    JOHN MASON
          Let's take a moment of silent
          meditation as we prepare to hear from
          the 1991 - 1992 Hillfield University
          Student Government President, Quincy
          Collins.

TEARS stream down John Mason's face. As he turns around to face
QUINCY COLLINS, and the rest of the Pre-Alumni Association, his
composure is bipolar and emotionless.

Quincy Collins' (21), personality amazingly falls just a few steps short of a pet rock. Quincy wears glasses equally as un-amazing as his charisma. John Mason pokes a finger into QUINCY COLLINS' chest.

> JOHN MASON
> (to Quincy)
> I've got them. Try not to lose them.

John Mason outstretches his arms. Lawrence slips on John Mason's overcoat.

Lawrence gently touches John Mason on the HAND.

> LAWRENCE
> Your speech really moved me.

John Mason SMILES devilishly. Touches Lawrence softly on the hand.

> JOHN MASON
> As it should. Next year, the gimp will
> be gone, and I will be the Hillfield
> University Student Government
> President.

John Mason whips out a CIGAR from his coat pocket. He passionately sniffs it as he stares at Quincy, then stuffs it back into his pocket.

Quincy fumbles through a pile of NOTE-CARDS.

John Mason rolls his eyes at Quincy.

> QUINCY
> (reads)
> Be may that every year Freshmen
> Orientation exposes you to Hillfield
> traditions - Spirit Night, Chapel, the
> Block Party, and the Run - I encourage
> all of you to be not a number, but a
> member of an organization.
>
> The first day of class begins in two
> hours. Remember, a Hillfield Man must
> always-

> ALL FRESHMEN
> (patronizes)
> Be on time.

The Hill

                    QUINCY
        And to be on time means-

                  ALL FRESHMEN
                  (lackadaisical)
        To be fifteen minutes early.

                    QUINCY
        This concludes Orientation. Thank you
        very much. God bless. Goodnight.

                                        TIME CUT TO:

EXT. GRAVEYARD - DAY

Winston slyly approaches John Mason.

                    WINSTON
        John Mason
              (offers his hand)
        Winston Chamberlain. We became
        acquainted this summer at Oak Bluffs.

Winks.

John Mason sucks his teeth.

                    JOHN MASON
        Yes, I remember. Come to the first
        Pre-Alumni Association meeting and
        I'll introduce you to some of the
        family. Or you can drop by my room
        sometime. I'm the R.A. on the third
        floor of Smith Hall.

                                        CUT TO:

EXT. COLLEGE OF ARTS & SCIENCES - DAY

Students tote BOOK BAGS and scurry into the building.

INT. CLASSROOM - DAY

Adam sits in a classroom along with T.J., Winston, and twenty other
students-two of which are girls (Liesl and Kaneisha).

DR. MFUME (45), an estranged female professor extraordinaire, sits
quietly as she stares at the students and listens to their chatter.

As the students realize that someone watches them, the banter
decrescendos to an uncomfortable silence. Dr. Mfume rises and
addresses the chalkboard. She scrawls out in letters whose height
is equal to that of the chalkboard:

A   F   R   I   K   A

Faces the class.

>   DR. MFUME
>   Afrika.

>   WINSTON
>   I think you spelled it wrong.

The class SNICKERS.

>   DR. MFUME
>   Says who?

Winston removes a PAPERBACK BOOK from his backpack.

>   WINSTON
>   Webster's dictionary.

>   DR. MFUME
>   And who wrote it?

>   WINSTON
>   Noah Webster.

>   DR. MFUME
>   And where is he from?

SILENCE.

>   DR. MFUME
>   Hello, my name is Dr. Mfume, and this
>   is "The History of Civilization."
>   Welcome.

>   TIME CUT TO:

INT. CLASSROOM - DAY

Dr. Mfume sits on top of her desk as she reviews the COURSE SYLLABUS.
The students peruse their own personal copies of it.

                    DR. MFUME
          At the conclusion of this course, each
          of you will hand in a 50-page essay
          dealing with The Destruction of Afrikan
          Civilization.

People MOAN.

                    DR. MFUME
          We'll discuss it further on Wednesday.
          Class dismissed.

Adam leans over towards' T.J.'s desk.

                    ADAM
          Do you want to hit the library with me?

                    T.J.
          No, I have to go to Financial Aid. My
          funds still haven't been dispersed.

Liesl brushes up against Adam.

                    LIESL
          I'll go with you.

Smiles.

                                        CUT TO:

EXT. STREET - DAY

Adam and Liesl walk along the sidewalk towards the steps of
HILLFIELD LIBRARY. A SPEAKER propped up in the window of a BOARDING
HOUSE blasts the beats of a LIVE MIX. A crowd of brothers stands
in front of the house taking turns freestyling rhymes on the mic.
Several onlookers seated on the library steps bob their heads to
the beats while smacking on WING SPECIALS in STYROFOAM PLATES.

                                        DISSOLVE TO:

INT. LIBRARY - DAY

Adam and Liesl sit at a table as they flip through books. The library
is full of courting brothers and sisters, but Adam and Liesl are
the only ones who actually have books.

                    ADAM
          So, what do you wanna' be when you grow
          up?

Adam looks into Liesl's eyes.

> LIESL
> I wanna' be a lawyer. And you?

> ADAM
> I want to make a difference. If one will
> lead, many will follow.
> > (takes Liesl by the hand)
> Trust me.

INSERT

King James Bible - Genesis Chapter 2

> OVERLAY:

INT. BLACK ROOM - DAY

There are three dark stages in triangle formation. Adam #1 sits at a table in the middle of the frame as he flips through pages in a pile of books. Adam #2 walks to the first stage.

A SPOTLIGHT illuminates Stage #1, located in the lower left hand corner of the frame.

John Mason, Hosea, and Osiris stare at an APPLE TREE in the middle of the stage. They point at the FRUIT, hesitant to take a piece.

> ADAM (V.O.)
> **Genesis, Chapter 2, Verses 16 & 17.** And
> the LORD God commanded the man, saying,
> of every tree of the garden thou mayest
> freely eat:
>
> But of the tree of the knowledge of good
> and evil, thou shalt not eat of it: for
> in the day that thou eatest thereof thou
> shalt surely die.

The lights go down on stage #1. Adam walks over to stage #2. It is illuminated by a SPOTLIGHT.

Adam #1 opens another book.

OVERLAY

Introduction to Afrikan Civilizations - Chapter 6

Quincy, Cleo, and Pete sit together with their legs folded in the right front corner of the stage. Three Preachers; Evers, Morgan, and Ronald; sit together with their legs folded at the back stage. Kareem, Jonas, and Dashon sit together with their legs folded on the left side of the stage.

> ADAM
> The first Spanish and Portuguese
> explorers found colonies of Black men
> on the eastern coasts of South and
> Central America, and in Yucatan and
> Nicaragua.

The LIGHTS GO DOWN on stage #2.

Adam #2 walks over to stage #3. A SPOTLIGHT illuminates the stage.

Osiris sits on a HORSE while he holds a LANCE.

> ADAM
> The Moors had a thriving empire
> spanning from Spain to Persia for over
> 500 years.
>
> The word "Moor" literally means
> "Black," so the Moorish people were the
> Black people.
>
> In medieval time the name Moor was not
> restricted to the inhabitants of
> Morocco, but it was customary to refer
> to all Afrikans as Moors.

> CUT TO:

BLACK SCREEN

A SCROLL of old parchment opens and rolls down the left side of the screen and down across the bottom of the screen from left to right. The last portion of the scroll reveals:

> **...THE ISSUES...**

> CUT TO:

INT. CIRCUS - TRAPEZE - NIGHT

A HOODED MAN dressed in a RED SATIN ROBE stands on the right side
of the screen on a high wire while he holds a rope, which descends
from somewhere above. TRAPEZE ARTIST #1 swings from the left of the
screen to the right. Lands. Disappears from the frame.

TRAPEZE ARTIST #2 swings from left to right, lands, and disappears.
As the Trapeze moves towards Trapeze Artist #3, the Hooded Man
pulls the rope. The trapeze raises. Trapeze Artist #3 misses, and
flails his limbs as he falls out of the frame.

A word appears in the center of the screen:

<u>**COLOR**</u>

CUT TO:

INT. BOXING RING - NIGHT

Lawrence, dressed in an ALL BLACK SUIT AND TIE, faces Terrell,
dressed in an ALL WHITE SUIT AND TIE. They both wear BOXING GLOVES.
The floor of the boxing ring is covered with a FLAT MAP OF THE WORLD.

Adam stands between them. Adam wears a LETTERMAN SWEATER, which
reads: "THE HILL." He stares directly at the camera.

Chancellor Dix and Dean Richards sit ringside at the judges' table
respectively garbed in a GENERAL'S AND ADMIRAL'S MILITARY DRESS.

Liesl, dressed as a ring card girl, walks into the center of the
frame and holds up a RING CARD which reads:

(SUIT - VS. - SUIT)

Adam smacks the gloves of Lawrence and Terrell.

As Lawrence and Terrell bump gloves, a BELL RINGS.

CUT TO:

SPLIT SCREEN

The screen is split into four screens.

SCREEN 1 - CONTINUOUS

EXT. CHAPEL - DAY

Adam enters a side door at the rear of the chapel.

The Hill

CUT TO:

INT. CHAPEL - OFFICE - DAY

Evers sits behind a desk in a small office. A nameplate on the desk reads:

VICE-CHANCELLOR OF CHAPEL ASSISTANTS

Adam takes a seat in front of Evers desk. Evers talks to him.

> ADAM (V.O.)
> School starts off with a bang. Evers
> makes me his assistant, but I soon found
> out why he's so interested in
> befriending me.

SPLIT SCREEN:

SCREEN 2 - CONTINUOUS

INT. SPRINGFIELD UNIVERSITY FINANCIAL AID OFFICE - DAY

Liesl searches through records on a computer. She writes several names on a POST-IT NOTE. Walks over to the file cabinet. Searches through files.

> ADAM (V.O.)
> Liesl works in the Financial Aid Office
> at Springfield University. Evers is
> looking for the name of a needy girl who
> does not have a scholarship. And he
> finds one.

Liesl reads from a file.

> LIESL
> (finishes Adam's phrase)
> Duh, Kaneisha Jackson-Washington.

SPLIT SCREEN:

SCREEN 1 - CONTINUOUS

INT. CHAPEL - OFFICE - DAY

Evers sits behind his desk.

                         EVERS
                    (finishes Liesl's
                    phrase)
          Perfect.

Kaneisha sits in a chair in front of Evers' desk. Evers provides
her with a mini sermonette.

                         EVERS
               My Mom and the Chancellor of
               Springfield were soro's who crossed
               together on the same line at
               Springfield.

                                        SPLIT SCREEN:

SCREEN 3 - CONTINUOUS

EXT. THE QUAD - NIGHT

Kaneisha bumps into John Mason. She faints and falls into his arms.
John carries her into his dormitory.

                         ADAM (V.O.)
               Evers promises Kaneisha that she will
               receive financial aid if she supports
               her Progressive Hillfield preachers in
               their hour of need.

                                        CUT TO:

INT. JOHN MASON'S DORM ROOM - NIGHT

Kaneisha lies on the bed. John Mason brings her a GLASS OF WATER
and an ASPIRIN. She smiles. John makes a place for himself to sleep
on the floor.

                                        CUT TO:

INT. SECURITY OFFICE - DAY

A CAMPUS POLICE OFFICER leads Kaneisha into the office. She cries,
covered in a blanket.

                         ADAM (V.O.)
               Come morning, she calls security,
               hysterical, proclaiming-

                         KANEISHA
                 John Mason raped me!

                                           SPLIT SCREEN:

SCREEN 4 - CONTINUOUS

INT. CHANCELLOR'S OFFICE - DAY

John Mason sits at a long table before a disciplinary committee,
which consists of Chancellor Dix and FOUR OTHERS. They shake their
heads.

                         ADAM (V.O.)
                 Hillfield does not hesitate to give
                 John a candy bar, comic book, and a bus
                 ride back home.

                    COMMITTEE MEMBER JANE
                 He was such a nice boy.

                                           SPLIT SCREEN:

SCREEN 1 - CONTINUOUS

INT. CHAPEL OFFICE - DAY

Adam hands Evers a piece of paper.

                         ADAM (V.O.)
                 And of course, Kaneisha is justly
                 rewarded. Here's that letter you asked
                 me to write to the Chancellor of
                 Springfield for Kaneisha.

Evers takes the letter, balls it up, and shoots a three-pointer with
it into a TRASH CAN.

ALL FOUR SPLIT SCREENS REVOLVE TO REVEAL A SINGLE IMAGE SPREAD
ACROSS ALL FOUR SCREENS

INT. JOHN MASON'S DORM ROOM - DAY

Several BOXES and SUITCASES are stacked up next to the door.
Lawrence helps John pack a TRUNK. Their HANDS accidentally touch
each other.

A beat.

They gaze into each other's eyes.

                                            CUT TO:

EXT. THE QUAD - DAY

Evers sits on the steps of his dorm as he watches John Mason and
Lawrence through the window of John's dorm room.

P.O.V. - EVERS

John and Lawrence stand next to each other in a long embrace. They
break apart. Lawrence leaves the room.

Evers smiles. Lights a cigar. Walks towards John's Dorm. John exits
the building as he carries a box. John walks across the Quad. Evers
intentionally bumps into John.

                                      CROSS CUT TO:

INT. JOHN MASON'S DORM ROOM - DAY

A single tear rolls down Lawrence's cheek.

P.O.V. - LAWRENCE

Evers takes a drag from his cigar and forms his lips like a kiss.
Blows smoke in John's face.

END SPLIT SCREEN

                                            CUT TO:

EXT. SMITH HALL - DAY

Students enter the building.

                                            CUT TO:

INT. SMITH HALL - MEETING ROOM - DAY

The Pre-Alumni Association officers are seated at a long table
before the other members of the Pre-Alumni Association. Terrell is
seated at the center of the table. Lawrence is to his right.

                    TERRELL
          In reference to the recent tragedy of
          events, I apologize, and promise that
          this administration will have no
          further such faults.

          Admittedly, our reputation has been
          tarnished, but the Hillfield
          Pre-Alumni Association has a rich
          tradition of leadership at this great
          institution.

          I am positive that our history speaks
          for itself and we will recover.

          We had all hoped that John would take
          the helm of next year's Student
          Government as so many of our Premieres
          of the Pre-Alumni Association past.

          I would like to take this time to fully
          acknowledge that I will run for the 1992
          - 1993 Presidency of the Hillfield
          University Student Government. And I
          will win, and I will bring honor to the
          men of Pre-Alumni.

The Pre-Alumni members applaud.

                    TERRELL
          This meeting is adjourned.

The Pre-Alumni officers rise. Lawrence fishes through a briefcase.
Terrell leans over to Lawrence. Puts his arm around him.

                    TERRELL
          Lawrence, I want you to be my Chief of
          Staff.

                    LAWRENCE
               (troubled)
          Sure, anything.

                                        CUT TO:

EXT. HILLFIELD HALL - DAY

HUNDREDS OF STUDENTS wait in an endless line stemming from the front of the building.

A makeshift sign taped to the front doors reads: FINANCIAL AID.

T.J. is stuck in the middle of the line.

INT. CHANCELLOR'S OFFICE - DAY

Chancellor Dix sits behind his desk as he reviews a file labeled: "LAWRENCE JEFFRIES." BAROQUE CLASSICAL MUSIC plays softly in the background.

[A SCENE FROM A SOLDIER'S STORY PLAYS ON HIS:]

TELEVISION

INT. BAR - NIGHT

Sergeant Waters and Private Wilkie turn away from the bar and watch C.J. play his guitar and sing the blues.

> SERGEANT WATERS
> My daddy told me we got to turn our backs
> on these kind, Wilkie. Close our ranks
> to the chitterlings, collard greens,
> cornbread style.

END TELEVISION

The INTERCOM BEEPS.

Chancellor Dix turns off the television with a REMOTE CONTROL.

> MRS. THOMPSON (O.S.)
> Chancellor Dix? Lawrence Jeffries is
> here to see you, sir.

Chancellor Dix pushes a button on the telephone.

> CHANCELLOR DIX
> Send him in, please.

Lawrence timidly steps into the office.

Chancellor Dix stands as he faces a wall with portraits of all the past Hillfield University Chancellors. The majority of men in the portraits have light complexions.

Chancellor Dix, as his back faces Lawrence, snaps his fingers and points to a seat before his desk. Lawrence takes the cue.

Chancellor Dix walks along the wall of portraits. He stops and looks up at one.

> CHANCELLOR DIX
> The Reverend Doctor Samuel T. Bennett
> - Bishop. Hillfield University
> Chancellor 1892 to 1914. Hillfield
> University Student Government
> President 1873 to 1874.

Chancellor Dix walks along the wall. Stops at another portrait.

> CHANCELLOR DIX
> Dr. Nathaniel C. Thompson - Mayor.
> Hillfield University Chancellor 1941
> to 1957. Student Government President
> 1919 to 1920.

Chancellor Dix takes a few more steps. Admires another portrait.

> CHANCELLOR DIX
> Dr. William H. Lewis - CEO. Hillfield
> University Chancellor 1963 to 1978.
> Student Government President 1933 to
> 1934.

Chancellor Dix peruses the wall.

> CHANCELLOR DIX
> A handsome lot, weren't they?

Chancellor Dix stares at a portrait of himself.

> CHANCELLOR DIX
> I too was a Hillfield University
> Student Government President.

Chancellor Dix faces Lawrence.

                         CHANCELLOR DIX
          Hillfield University has a long, proud,
          rich history of tradition. I understand
          that you yourself have aspirations in
          academia.

          Earlier today Terrell announced his
          candidacy for next year's Student
          Government Presidency.

          The Hillfield University Student
          Government President is a position of
          great power, prestige, and prosperity.
          Freshmen year, you and Terrell were
          roommates.

          You're like brothers. You know things
          about each other. Terrell has a 2.9
          G.P.A., but you have a 3.7.

          You work hard, don't you? But it only
          takes a 2.7 to run for Student
          Government President. Doesn't seem
          fair, does it. However, Terrell is
          quite well liked, but-

Chancellor Dix innocently removes a small BROWN PAPER BAG from his
briefcase.

                         CHANCELLOR DIX
          It seems like he's been getting quite
          a bit of sun lately.

Chancellor Dix removes a ruler from the bag.

                         CHANCELLOR DIX
          And what is he putting in his hair these
          days? It's very robust.

Chancellor Dix sticks the ruler in his desk drawer.

                         CHANCELLOR DIX
          Did he run track in high school?
                    (gestures towards his
                     own nose)
          Looks like he can supply quite a bit of
          air to his lungs.

Ponders a beat.

>   CHANCELLOR DIX
>   Doesn't your family own a summer home
>   in Sag Harbor? I have one myself at
>   Martha's Vineyard. And didn't you grow
>   up in Jack and Jill?
>
>   Terrell doesn't know Jack from Jill and
>   he's never even been to Sag Harbor or
>   the Vineyard. Do you get what I'm
>   saying?
>
>   Terrell is a nice boy, but he's not like
>   you and me. A real man. He's not our kind
>   of people.

Lawrence stares at Chancellor Dix.

Chancellor Dix faces the wall of portraits.

>   THEN:

Violently shoves his computer off his desk, which sends it into the
floor with a CRASH.

>   CHANCELLOR DIX
>   (enraged)
>   And there will not be a pick ninny
>   Student Government President on my
>   watch. Never, not ever! This is your
>   responsibility!

Chancellor Dix turns his back to Lawrence and faces the window.

A beat.

As he maintains eye contact, Chancellor Dix reaches behind him and
flips open a BOX OF CIGARS on his desktop.

Lawrence stares at the cigars.

Chancellor Dix reaches into his coat pocket and flips open a
PLATINUM LIGHTER, outstretches his arm, and ignites it.

Lawrence's hands tremble as he takes a CUTTER and clips the tip of
the cigar. Slips the cigar in his mouth. Leans forward to light it.

Chancellor Dix flips the lighter closed, and stuffs it back into
his coat pocket.

                    CHANCELLOR DIX
          Good day, sir.

Lawrence coughs as he takes a drag from the cigar. He heads for the
door.

                    CHANCELLOR DIX
          And get some new glasses.

Chancellor Dix pushes a button on his desk phone, which activates
his intercom.

                    CHANCELLOR DIX
                 (into intercom)
          Mrs. Thompson, get me the Swiss
          Corporation on the line.

                                                  CUT TO:

INT. CLEO WALLINGFORD'S DORM ROOM - NIGHT

CLEO WALLINGFORD (20), an ambitious justice on the student court,
sits at a desk as he reads through a pile of BOOKS. His dorm door
is propped open. On the door is a sign, which reads: "Resident
Advisor."

Lawrence steps into the doorway. Raps on the door. He wears a new
pair of HIP GLASSES with ULTRA THIN LENSES.

                    LAWRENCE
          Studying?

                    WALLINGFORD
          Yup.

                    LAWRENCE
          You work hard, don't you?

                    WALLINGFORD
                 (ignoring)
          This is not your floor.

                         LAWRENCE
          It was a shame when you got passed over
          for Chief Justice. You work the
          hardest. Do well in school, too.

          Some folks don't put nearly as much
          effort in their studies, as they do
          campaigning, yet they seem to reap all
          the rewards.

Wallingford stares down into his books.

                         LAWRENCE
          I appreciate a hard worker who is not
          a punk. So does Chancellor Dix.

Wallingford looks up from his book and directly into Lawrence's
EYES.

                         WALLINGFORD
          Close the door.

Lawrence closes the DOOR.

                                                   CUT TO:

EXT. DEAN RICHARD'S OFFICE - NIGHT

Several men from The Hill congregate outside, giddy as school
"girlz".

The marquee reads:

THE HILL NIGHT

                                                   CUT TO:

INT. CAR - NIGHT

Evers sits behind the steering wheel and Adam is in the passenger's
seat. The car is parked three blocks away from Debra's Nightclub.

Ever's LIGHTS a CIGAR.

Adam fans the SMOKE and coughs.

                         ADAM
          Must you do that?

Evers laughs. He rolls down the windows. He stares at Debra's Nightclub.

Adam traces his eye line.

                    ADAM
              (about Debra's)
          What is that? The place to be?

                    EVERS
              (smiles)
          Depends. That's Debra's. It's where
          many men from The Hill meet their
          boyfriends at 1:00 after they drop off
          their girlfriends at 12:00.

                    ADAM
              (uncomfortable)
          Wait a minute, now. You're not, uh, and
          I hope that you don't think I'm uh.

Evers takes a drag from his cigar.

                    EVERS
          No, I'm not. I'm fucking appalled. It's
          a God damn blasphemous sin. They should
          all die.

                    ADAM
          Well, on the other hand, there's no need
          to go to extremes. Some people are
          different. It doesn't mean that they're
          going to make us be different with them.

                    EVERS
          That's not what I'm talking about. The
          same people that you see frolicking and
          twirling in there are the same people
          that will relentlessly crucify someone
          else publicly for something they do
          privately.

          Be who you're going to be, but don't be
          fake and punish other people for it.

Evers extinguishes his cigar in the ASHTRAY.

                                        CUT TO:

INT. STUDENT COURTROOM - DAY

Evers and Adam enter the courtroom and take a seat in the back of the courtroom. All of the disciples of ANKH sit in the back of the courtroom on the left.

The Chapel Assistants sit in the back of the courtroom on the left. The Pre-alumni Members are split on two sides of the front of the courtroom: those on the right with Terrell and those on the left with Lawrence.

BAILIFF BOB stands.

                    BAILIFF BOB
          All rise.

The CHIEF JUSTICE and SIX JUSTICES, one of which is Cleo Wallingford, enter the room and take their seats at the front of the courtroom.

                    CHIEF JUSTICE
          We've heard both parties speak. After
          careful review of both points of view,
          we have decided that the minimum G.P.A.
          to run for the Student Government
          Presidency shall hither be 3.0. Court
          is adjourned.

The Chief Justice SLAMS a GAVEL.

Lawrence and Cleo Wallingford lock eyes. Wallingford nods. Lawrence returns the nod.

                    TERRELL
          This is bullshit.

Terrell pushes through the crowd towards Lawrence.

                    TERRELL
          They smile in your face - back stabbers.
          And do you really think you'll be the
          next Student Government President?

                    LAWRENCE
          No. I know I'll be.

Terrell tries to bash Lawrence in the lip, but the Pre-alumni members hold Terrell back.

                         TERRELL
                You ain't shit. You ain't never been
                shit. And you ain't never gonna' be
                shit.

Lawrence sticks a CIGAR in his mouth. He whips out a MATCH and LIGHTS
it off the side of Terrell's cheek. IGNITES his cigar. Takes a puff.
Blows SMOKE in Terrell's face.

Terrell snatches the cigar from Lawrence's mouth. Breaks it in half.
Throws it in Lawrence's face.

                         TERRELL
                Watch your back.

Terrell storms off.

Evers looks at Adam.

Adam fans away a bit of smoke that lingers. Coughs.

                         EVERS
                End of round 1.

A BELL RINGS.

                                            CUT TO:

INT. LIBRARY - DAY

Liesl sits at a table as she flips through BOOKS. Adam spots her
from afar and takes a seat next to her. Adam places his BOOK BAG
on the table.

                         ADAM
                How's your paper coming along?

Liesl gets up. Adam grabs Liesl.

                         ADAM
                Wait!

                         LIESL
                I have nothing to say to you.

                         ADAM
                I'm sorry about what happened to
                Kaneisha.

                    LIESL
          Sorry? What you did to Kaneisha was
          really foul. She was a good girl.

                    ADAM
          Evers just asked her to distract John
          Mason. How were we supposed to know that
          he was a rapist?

                    LIESL
          Using people - is that how you plan to
          make your difference?

Adam takes Liesl by the hand.

                    ADAM
          Evers has given me the opportunity to
          really make difference at this place.
          And, I promise, the first difference
          I'll make is with him. Trust me.

Liesl gives in.

Adam caresses her shoulder.

                    ADAM
          That's my girl. I promise if I get in
          too deep, I'll get out.

                    LIESL
          Or drown.

Adam reaches into his book bag, and removes a stack of BOOKS.

INSERT

King James Bible - Genesis Chapter 4

                              DISSOLVE TO:

INT. BLACK ROOM - DAY

There are three dark stages in triangle formation. Adam #1 sits at
a table in the middle of the frame as he flips through pages in a
pile of books. Adam #2 walks to the first stage.

A SPOTLIGHT illuminates Stage #1, located in the lower left hand
corner of the frame.

Lawrence and Terrell, dressed in SUITS, hunch over with HOES as they till an imaginary field. In classic Greek Theater fashion, Lawrence pantomimes striking Terrell with his hoe. Terrell pantomimes death.

> ADAM (V.O.)
> **Genesis, Chapter 4, Verse 8.** And Cain talked with Abel his brother: and it came to pass, when they were in the field, that Cain rose up against Abel his brother, and slew him.

The lights go down on stage #1. Adam walks over to stage #2. It is illuminated by a SPOTLIGHT.

Adam #1 opens another book.

OVERLAY

From Slavery To Freedom - Chapter 8

Three students stand on an OLYMPIC WINNERS platform. On the Gold Medal spot John Mason wears an APRON and holds a TRAY. On the silver medal spot is Hosea hunched over as he holds a HORSESHOE and a HAMMER. On the third platform is Osiris who kneels with a BUSHEL OF COTTON.

> ADAM
> There were typically three types of slaves on the plantation: house slaves, field slaves, and skilled slaves.
>
> The house slaves, usually lighter in complexion, were often the illegitimate children of the slave owners. They were frequently treated better.

The LIGHTS GO DOWN on stage #2.

Adam #1 opens another book.

Adam #2 walks over to stage #3. It is illuminated by a SPOTLIGHT.

Pete swings a BULL WHIP at T.J. and Winston. They try to shield themselves from the whip.

                    ADAM
          There was another type of slave on the
          plantation called the driver, or "head
          driver." It was the driver's
          responsibility to help the overseer
          make the other slaves work harder.

The LIGHTS GO DOWN on stage #3.

                                        CUT TO:

BLACK SCREEN

GRUNTS. A CHAIN is pulled by both ends. One link stretches, then
breaks. The link flies toward the camera in slow motion. It stops,
then rotates to reveal the word:

                         AFRIKA

                                        CUT TO:

INT. BOXING RING - NIGHT

BOXING RING. Uniformly dressed PREACHERS (Hosea, Evers, Morgan, &
Ronald) who wear CLERGY COLLARS stand on one side of the screen while
uniformly dressed AFRIKANS (Osiris, Kareem, Jonas, & Dashon) stand
on the other side in gowns and combat boots. Both the Preachers and
Afrikans wear BOXING GLOVES. The floor of the boxing ring is covered
with a FLAT WORLD MAP.

Adam stands in the center of the ring. He wears a LETTERMAN SWEATER,
which reads: "THE HILL." Adam stares directly at the camera.

Chancellor Dix and Dean Richards sit ringside at the judges' table
respectively garbed in a GENERAL'S AND ADMIRAL'S MILITARY DRESS.

Liesl, dressed as a ring card girl, walks into the center of the
ring and holds up a RING CARD which reads:

                (PREACHERS -VS. - AFRIKANS)

Adam smacks the gloves of Evers and Osiris. As all fighters bump
the gloves of a fighter from an opposing camp, a BELL RINGS.

                                        WIPE RIGHT TO:

A SLIGHTLY SMALLER THAN TV ASPECT RATIO FRAME

SUPERIMPOSE - CONTINUOUS

A translucent GOLD overlay with an ANKH SYMBOL. The ankh part is clear.

EXT. ANDERSON HALL - NIGHT

CARDBOARD and DUCT TAPE serve as a renegade patch on BROKEN WINDOW.

> ADAM (V.O.)
> The Afrikans have the worst dorm on
> campus. It isn't like the projects, it
> is the projects.

                                        CUT TO:

INT. ANDERSON HALL - BETWEEN THE WALLS - NIGHT

An OLD RUSTY PIPE EXPLODES, which spews CHUNKS OF ICE and GUSHES WATER onto a FRAYED POWER LINE. SPARKS fly and FIRE embroils.

> ADAM (V.O.)
> As it gets cold, the pipes burst, and
> an electrical fire starts.

                                        CUT TO:

EXT. ANDERSON HALL - NIGHT

OVERWEIGHT and PINT-SIZED Hillfield University SECURITY GUARDS bump into to each other as they SQUIRT FIRE EXTINGUISHERS at roaring FLAMES at the top of the building. Osiris and the Disciples of ANKH stand outside in the Quad covered in SOOT as they shiver in their BOXER SHORTS.

> ADAM (V.O.)
> The keystone cops put out the fire, but
> it's one too many frozen Afrikans for
> Osiris to let it go by idly.

                                        WIPE UP TO:

SUPERIMPOSE - CONTINUOUS

A translucent RED overlay with a BLACK POWER FIST. The fist part is clear.

INT. NEWS VAN - DAY

A conservative Afrikan-American woman, MARSHA COHEN, fixes her hair
and applies MAKE-UP.

> ADAM (V.O.)
> The anchorwoman from the Channel 6 news
> is the scheduled speaker at the next
> Assembly.

                                                            CUT TO:

EXT. HILLFIELD HALL - DAY

Marsha Cohen stands nearby in front of Hillfield Chapel with her
camera crew. She is greeted by hundreds of students, POLICE CARS,
and FLASHING LIGHTS. The Disciples of ANKH are chained to the doors
of Hillfield Hall.

> ADAM (V.O.)
> When she arrives with her camera crew
> to do an uplifting piece about the men
> of The Hill, she's met by several crazed
> Afrikans who have taken over Hillfield
> Hall.

A SMALL FRAME CRAWLS RIGHT TO LEFT ACROSS THE TOP OF THE SCREEN.

Osiris speaks into a MEGAPHONE.

> OSIRIS
> No justice, no peace!

A SMALL FRAME CRAWLS LEFT TO RIGHT ACROSS THE BOTTOM OF THE SCREEN.

Osiris holds up a picture of Chancellor Dix and Dean Richards.

> OSIRIS
> Chancellor Dix and Dean Richards are
> Uncle Toms!!

A SMALL FRAME CRAWLS FROM THE TOP OF THE SCREEN TO THE BOTTOM.

Osiris waves a RUBBER PENIS.

> OSIRIS
> Dix has been a dick!

A SMALL FRAME CRAWLS FROM THE RIGHT OF THE SCREEN TO THE LEFT.

Osiris throws COTTON BALLS into the crowd.

> OSIRIS
> We wish we weren't in Dixie!

A SMALL FRAME GROWS FROM THE CENTER OF THE MAIN FRAME.

Osiris burns the picture of Chancellor Dix and Dean Richards.

> OSIRIS
> The last thing we need is more Hill
> Niggaz!!!

Marsha Cohen breaks through the crowd with her camera crew to insure that she is in the SPOTLIGHT.

> ADAM (V.O.)
> Osiris has planned well. With their
> dorm in piss poor shape, he has all the
> evidence on live television to back him
> up.
>
> The administration can't touch him, or
> at least he thinks so. Makes you wonder
> if he started the fire himself.

Osiris looks at the camera and WINKS.

WIPE DOWN TO:

SUPERIMPOSE - CONTINUOUS

A translucent GREEN overlay with a PEACE SIGN. The peace sign part is clear.

EXT. HILLFIELD HALL - TELEVISION FRAME - DAY

Chancellor Dix and Dean Richards stand with Marsha Cohen as they address America. Chancellor Dix and Dean Richards have shitty grins on their faces.

> ADAM (V.O.)
> Chancellor Dix does the buck and the
> whip dance for the camera, sure to show
> all his pearly white teeth, promising
> the revolutionary Afrikans-

The Hill

                    CHANCELLOR DIX
            No recourse and a new dorm.

CHEERS!!!

Dean Richards makes EYE CONTACT with Evers. They both nod.

                    ADAM (V.O.)
            But once the camera crews go, and all
            is said and done, the hourglass of
            Osiris' life at The Hill is overturned
            and his sands of time run thin.

END SLIGHTLY SMALLER THAN TV ASPECT RATIO

                                        CUT TO:

EXT. THE QUAD - DAY

Osiris stands on the steps of Anderson Hall with the Disciples of
ANKH lined up behind him. He addresses a crowd with his megaphone.
A Disciple plays THE HILL MAIN THEME on a stereo in the window of
Anderson Hall.

                    OSIRIS
            They thought that they could keep us
            down.

                    CROWD
            No!

                    OSIRIS
            They thought that they could keep us in
            the cold.

                    CROWD
            No!

                    OSIRIS
            They thought we would just give up.

                    CROWD
            No!

                    OSIRIS
            But, they couldn't keep us down!!!

                                    CROSS CUT TO:

INT. DEAN RICHARD'S OFFICE - DAY

Evers sits in a chair in front of Dean Richards' desk. Dean Richards has his back to Evers as Dean Richards peers out of his window. Dean Richards observes Osiris as Osiris addresses the crowd.

                                        CROSS CUT TO:

EXT. THE QUAD - DAY

Terrell and his Pre-alumni followers observe Osiris from the steps of Smith Hall.

Osiris holds up his STAFF.

                    OSIRIS
          There were three types of slaves on the
          plantations. House slaves, Field
          slaves, and skilled slaves.

          Many of the house slaves, mostly
          half-breeds, some with the master's
          blood running through their veins, were
          down for the cause.

          But, the question is, <u>whose</u> cause were
          they down for?

CHEERS.

                                        CROSS CUT TO:

INT. DEAN RICHARD'S OFFICE - DAY

Dean Richards continues to peer out of his window.

                    DEAN RICHARDS
          Goddamn Afrikans.

Dean Richards turns to face Evers.

                    DEAN RICHARDS
          I was ordained when I turned 18 years
          old. The Reverend Doctor Frederick T.
          Hillfield was ordained at 18 years old,
          too. Hillfield University was founded
          by preachers; not by Afrikans, not by
          suits.

                                        CROSS CUT TO:

The Hill

EXT. THE QUAD - DAY

Morgan and the Chapel Assistants observe Osiris from the steps of Packard Hall.

Osiris waves a WAD OF MONEY.

> OSIRIS
> Chancellor Dix and Dean Richards have already got theirs and don't give a damn if we ever get ours.
>
> In the 60's our parents asked for integration, but what the White man gave us was assimilation.
>
> Instead of mixing in with their culture, we were forced to adopt theirs and lose our own. Chancellor Dix and Dean Richards, have assimilated, adopted, and sold out.

                                        CROSS CUT TO:

INT. DEAN RICHARD'S OFFICE - DAY

Dean Richards points out of the window.

> DEAN RICHARDS
> The suits would like you to think that it was their half-breed ancestors of the slave masters that started this institution.
>
> That may be true at some other schools, but it's not true at this one. It was preachers and the church.

Dean Richards SLAMS his FIST on his desk.

> DEAN RICHARDS
> It's time we take this institution back!

                                        CUT TO BLACK:

EXT. THE QUAD - DAY

Osiris waves a PAMPHLET at the crowd.

                    OSIRIS
          During slavery times, the White man
          raped our mothers, and today Chancellor
          Dix and Dean Richards are raping our
          brothers. I'm mad as hell, and I'm not
          going to take it any more.

                                        CROSS CUT TO:

INT. DEAN RICHARD'S OFFICE - DAY

Dean Richards sits in his chair. Glances out of the window.

                    DEAN RICHARDS
          You can either be part of the problem
          or part of the solution.

Dean Richards flips open a box of cigars. Leans back in his chair.

                    OSIRIS (O.S.)
          The preachers and the suits couldn't be
          happier than to maintain the status
          quo. Morgan, Lawrence, Evers,
          Terrell-all sellouts and the minions of
          an oppressive administration.

Evers takes a cigar from the box. Dean Richards whips out a lighter
and lights it.

                                        CROSS CUT TO:

EXT. THE QUAD - DAY

Osiris drops down to one knee.

                    OSIRIS (O.S.)
          Just as I brought justice to you today,
          I will bring justice to you tomorrow
          when you elect me, Osiris, the 1992 -
          1993 Hillfield University Student
          Government President.

PANDEMONIUM.

                    KAREEM
              (chants)
          'Siris! 'Siris! 'Siris!

The crowd catches on and chants along with Kareem.

The Hill

                                                          CUT TO:

INT. OSIRIS' DORM ROOM - NIGHT

An upside down half-burned AMERICAN FLAG hangs on one wall. A larger
than life size POSTER OF MALCOLM X "BY ANY MEANS NECESSARY" hangs
on another wall.

Osiris sits in chair along with Kareem and Jonas sit next to Osiris
amidst a meeting of the ANKH minds. They are all crowded around a
television set. They all smack on STYROFOAM containers filled with
WING SPECIALS.

Jonas has his ear glued to the phone. He listens to ELEVATOR STYLE
MUSIC. The phone BEEPS in his ear.

                                                          CUT TO:

TELEVISION

INT. NEWSROOM - DAY

Marsha Cohen delivers the news from a studio set.

                         MARSHA
               Following a dormitory fire, the men of
               The Hill protested today against poor
               building and grounds standards and
               questionable university policies and
               procedures.

EXT. CHAPEL - DAY

Osiris speaks into a megaphone. Kareem and Jonas stand chained next
to Osiris.

                         OSIRIS
               No justice, no peace.

END TELEVISION

INT. OSIRIS' DORM ROOM - DAY

Osiris, Kareem, and Jonas slap each other high five.

TELEVISION

EXT. STREET - NIGHT

RODNEY KING begs for mercy as LAPD officers beat him mercilessly
and pull on the chain around his neck.

                    MARSHA COHEN (O.S.)
               We just got this shocking footage of
               blatant police brutality from an
               amateur videographer in Los Angeles!

END TELEVISION

                                                  CUT TO:

INT. OSIRIS' DORM ROOM - NIGHT

Kareem turns down the television volume.

                    EVERYONE
               Damn!

                    KAREEM
               I can't believe this shit.

                    OSIRIS
               You can't believe that the pigs would
               beat a Black man, brother?

                    KAREEM
               No, I can't believe that someone
               finally got it on tape.

INT. ANDERSON HALL - HALLWAY - NIGHT

A PAY PHONE RINGS in the hallway. DISCIPLE DASHON (19), answers the
phone.

                    DISCIPLE DASHON
               Peace and Blessings.
                    (a beat)
               Who???

INT. OSIRIS DORM ROOM - NIGHT

The meeting of the minds is interrupted by a knock at the door.

                    OSIRIS
               See who it is.

The Hill

Jonas opens the door. It's Disciple DaShon.

> DISCIPLE DASHON
> Osiris, you have phone call on the pay
> phone.

> OSIRIS
> Tell them to call my room.

> DISCIPLE DASHON
> She said it rings and rings, but the
> voicemail won't pick up.

> OSIRIS
> Jonas, what did I tell you about not
> clicking over?

> JONAS
> I've been on hold for 15 minutes!

                                        CUT TO:

INT. ANDERSON HALL - HALLWAY - NIGHT

Osiris talks into the receiver at the pay phone.

> OSIRIS
> I told you never to call me on this
> number unless it's an emergency.

Dashon walks down the hallway towards the bathroom. He overhears
Osiris, becomes quite curious, and pauses in the bathroom doorway.
Osiris gives him a dirty look. Dashon disappears into the bathroom.

> OSIRIS
> (whispers)
> Yes, that was me on TV. I'm fine.
> Nothing has changed. In a couple of
> hours. Me too. Bye.

                                        CUT TO:

INT. ADAM'S DORM ROOM - NIGHT

T.J. IRONS a SHIRT on a HALF-SIZED IRONING BOARD propped up on top
of his desk. T.J. no longer has a Jheri curl. Winston sits on his
bed as he reads THE WALL STREET JOURNAL. Adam enters the room.

                        ADAM
                    (to T.J.)
            Did you ever get your financial aid
            straightened out?

                        T.J.
            They said that the Alumni Benevolent
            Fund ran out of money. I was supposed
            to get a full ride. I might not be able
            to come back next quarter.

An uncomfortable silence.

                        WINSTON
            The world needs ditch diggers.

Adam rolls his eyes at Winston.

T.J. lays his freshly ironed shirt across his bed.

                        ADAM
                    (to T.J.)
            Big date?

                        T.J.
            I'm going up yonder with some of the
            brothers who want to join ANKH to visit
            some sisters we met from Abigail
            Williams. My honey has a roommate.
            Wanna' roll with me?

                        ADAM
            What's Abigail Williams?

                        WINSTON
            It's an all girls school. A
            predominantly white all girls school.
            I suppose if my game was as feeble as
            yours, T.J., I too would necessitate a
            journey someplace where the female
            species was compelled to choose me due
            to lack of adequate choice.

Adam and Winston laugh. T.J. SQUIRTS them with WATER from the spray
button on the iron.

                        WINSTON
            Hey, my Journal!

                    ADAM
          I think I'll come. Besides, at least
          once a year we should all do some
          charity work.

                    WINSTON
          That's what the sisters at Abigail
          Williams will be singing when they see
          T.J.

Adam and Winston laugh. T.J. throws a WHOLE CUP OF WATER on Winston.

                                        CUT TO:

EXT. GIRL'S DORMITORY - NIGHT

WHITE GUYS AND GIRLS leave the dorm as they walk arm and arm and
hand in hand.

A LEFT-HAND.

A beat.

A tan right-hand from the same body slides a ring on the left-hand's
ring finger.

We hear the sound of a DEEP INHALE & EXHALE.

                                        CROSS CUT TO:

INT. GIRL'S DORMITORY - NIGHT

T.J. and Adam sit on a couch in the lobby. SEVERAL BROTHERS FROM
THE HILL talk in the lobby to AFRIKAN-AMERICAN GIRLS. Claude Dubose
(the pretty smooth boy with the Jag) is seated at a PIANO with a
crowd of sisters. He plays and sings along to STEVIE WONDER'S LOVE
SONG "A RIBBON IN THE SKY".

The elevator BEEPS. The elevator doors open.

                                        CROSS CUT TO:

Osiris smiles and outstretches his arms. It's his hand that now has
the ring on it.

                                        CROSS CUT TO:

A country girl, Lavette (18), steps out of the elevator. She's tar
black with a short Jheri Curl. Adam stands.

                         ADAM
          I'm leaving.

                         T.J.
                    (about her Jheri curl)
          Chill, I'm working on that.

Lavette and T.J. embrace.

                                        MATCH CUT TO:

INT. GIRLS DORM - NIGHT

Osiris in a long embrace with MAGGIE (20), a perky blonde-haired
green-eyed Barbie Doll type.

                         MAGGIE
          Danny, I was so worried about you.

                         OSIRIS
          I know.

Maggie runs her hands through Osiris' dreadlocks. Maggie's ring
finger has an identical ring to the one on Osiris' hand.

                         MAGGIE
          What's up with your hair, dude? You
          used to say that Bob Marley looked like
          a homeless man.

                         OSIRIS
          I know.

                                        CROSS CUT TO:

INT. LAVETTE'S DORM - LOBBY - NIGHT

T.J. takes Lavette by the hand and walks her over to Adam.

                         T.J.
          Adam, Lavette. Lavette, Adam.

                         LAVETTE
          He's cute. Ho-Ho will love him.

                         T.J.
          Ho-Ho?

                         LAVETTE
          That's her nickname.

Adam smiles.

>   T.J.
> And you were scared. I told you I had
> the hook up.

>   LAVETTE
> Sign-in, so you guys can come upstairs.

                                        CUT TO:

INT. LAVETTE'S DORM ROOM - NIGHT

Lavette opens the door. Adam and T.J. stand behind her.

                                  CROSS CUT TO:

INT. MAGGIE'S DORM ROOM - NIGHT

Osiris sits on the bed and rests his back against the wall.

                                  CROSS CUT TO:

INT. LAVETTE'S DORM ROOM - NIGHT

Ho-Ho (19), 400 lbs, four feet high, pimples, and glasses, shovels
Hostess "Ho-Ho's" into her mouth.

>   LAVETTE
> Ho-Ho, this is Adam.

>   HO-HO
> Whatever.

>   LAVETTE
> Don't worry, it takes a minute for her
> to warm-up.

Adam tries to escape, but T.J. has the door blocked.

>   LAVETTE
> Have a seat.

>   ADAM
> Close the door, T.J.

>   HO-HO
>   (stern)
> Underclassmen are not allowed to close
> their doors when men are in their rooms.

54.

Lavette seats Adam next to Ho-Ho on Ho-Ho's bed.

                         HO-HO
           If you touch me, I'll scream.

                         ADAM
           Funny, that's just what-

T.J. kicks Adam.

T.J. and Lavette sit on Lavette's bed.

A few of the Perspective Freshmen Disciples pass by the dorm room.

                    FRESHMEN VOICES
           What's up, Adam?

They LAUGH, then walk away.

                         ADAM
                    (mumbles to self)
           Yea though I walk through the valley of
           the shadow of death, he maketh me to lie
           down in green pastures.

                         LAVETTE
           What was that, Adam?

T.J. kicks Adam.

Ho-Ho continues to shovel "Ho-Ho's" into her mouth.

                         T.J.
                    (answers for Adam)
           Nothing.

THROUGH THE WINDOW - IN THE ADJACENT DORM

Maggie grabs a book from her desktop.

                         MAGGIE
           Look what mom sent me today.

                                        CROSS CUT TO:

INT. MAGGIE'S DORM ROOM - NIGHT

Maggie climbs onto the bed and leans her back against Osiris. She
puts Osiris arms around her. She flips through a PHOTO ALBUM.

                          MAGGIE
              Remember when we tried out for the
              cross-country team.

INSERT

A PICTURE of Osiris with a short un-stylish Afro and Maggie dressed
in sweats. They are both keeled over a bench as they hurl up lunch.

                          MAGGIE
              We Irish sure know how to drink.

                                        CROSS CUT TO:

INT. LAVETTE'S DORM ROOM - NIGHT

When in Rome, do as the Romans do.

                          ADAM
              Can I have a Ho-Ho?

                          HO-HO
              No.

Adam rises.

                          ADAM
              That's it.

Lavette grabs Adam.

                          LAVETTE
              Ho-Ho, show Adam your new video camera.

Ho-Ho tosses a camera bag at Adam.

                          HO-HO
              Break it. Buy it.

Adam tosses the bag back at Ho-Ho.

Adam peers:

THROUGH THE WINDOW

Osiris stares emotionless.

                              MAGGIE
          I can still remember prom night. Your
          mom was so excited. She kept calling me
          her favorite daughter. But your Dad
          really took the cake. You would have
          thought we were getting married that
          night.

END WINDOW

                              ADAM
          Oh, shit.

Ho-Ho smacks Adam on the cheek.

                              HO-HO
          Watch your language.

                              ADAM
          On second thought, let me take it for
          a test drive.

                              HO-HO
          Well, I never.

                              ADAM
          And you never will. The camera. Give me
          the camera.

Adam grabs the camera bag. He quickly lifts the video camera from
the bag, points it through the window, and presses a RECORD BUTTON.
A red light on the camera illuminates. A reflection of the red light
glistens on the DIAMOND of Adam's GOLD PINKY RING with the initials
"A.L.E." engraved on the it.

                                        CROSS CUT TO:

INT. MAGGIE'S DORM ROOM - NIGHT

INSERT

A picture of Osiris in a Tuxedo and Maggie in a prom dress. A gorgeous
ebony woman, OSIRIS' MOM (41), stands next to Maggie. A blonde
haired, green-eyed White man, OSIRIS' DAD (48), stands next to
Osiris.

                              MAGGIE
          You and your Dad can almost pass for
          twins. Same eyes. Same lips.

Osiris doesn't blink.

INSERT

A picture of Osiris and Maggie dressed in U2 paraphernalia. Osiris
holds a sleeping bag under his arm and Maggie sits on his shoulders
and cheers as she waves TWO TICKETS.

                    MAGGIE
          What about that time we skipped school
          and slept outside for the U2 concert.

                    OSIRIS
          Sunday, Bloody Sunday.

Maggie tosses aside the photo album. Turns to face Osiris.

                    MAGGIE
          I love you.

                    OSIRIS
          I Love you, too.

Osiris and Maggie embrace in a long passionate kiss while Osiris'
hand reaches and closes the WINDOW SHADE.

                                        CUT TO:

INT. EVERS DORM ROOM - NIGHT

Evers sits in his bed as he reads a copy of SUN TZU'S THE ART OF
WAR. The PHONE RINGS.

                    EVERS
          Evers. Osiris? You did? This changes
          things. You did the right thing. I'll
          take care of it.

                                        DISSOLVE TO:

EXT. CHAPEL - DAY

Straggling students race into the chapel.

                                        CUT TO:

INT. CHAPEL - DAY

Chapel Assistants, with CLIPBOARDS in hand, survey the rows of seats
CHECKING OFF the names of those who are and those who aren't present.

Hosea stands at the podium.

>   HOSEA
>   Today's assembly will be led by Osiris
>   and the Disciples of ANKH. I give to
>   you, Osiris.

Osiris walks onto the stage. The crowd cheers. The Disciples march
behind him and stand at attention in a straight line.

Hosea relinquishes the stage to Osiris.

INT. CHAPEL - OFFICE - DAY

Evers whispers to Morgan. Morgan, smiles, nods, then walks away.
Adam confronts Evers.

>   ADAM
>   Did you use the tape to blackmail Osiris
>   into not running for Student Government
>   President?

Evers puts his arm around Adam.

>   EVERS
>   Better.

INT. CHAPEL - DAY

Osiris is deep in his groove. He reads from a small book.

>   OSIRIS
>   Mentacide: The deliberate and
>   systematic destruction of a group or
>   individuals mind with the ultimate
>   objective of genocide.
>
>   The White Devils do this through their
>   media. By controlling the images we
>   see.

A screen slowly descends from the ceiling behind Osiris and the
Disciples.

                         OSIRIS
              Every time you turn on the television
              all you see is people of color
              committing crimes on the Police shows,
              being arrested on the news, or simply
              acting like a coon in June in a New
              Millennium Minstrel Show.
                         (points to screen)
              Observe.

Osiris buries his nose in his book.

INT. CHAPEL - BACK STAGE - DAY

Evers connects eyes with Morgan. They nod.

ON SCREEN / INSERT

A picture of Osiris and Maggie dressed in U2 paraphernalia. Osiris
holds a sleeping bag under his arm and Maggie sits on his shoulders
and cheers as she waves TWO TICKETS.

INT. CHAPEL - DAY

People snicker.

Osiris is puzzled, but doesn't look up at the screen.

Hosea confronts Evers.

                         HOSEA
              What's going on?

                         EVERS
              Justice.

ON SCREEN / INSERT

Maggie snuggles with Osiris.

                         MAGGIE
              What about that time we skipped school
              and slept outside for the U2 concert.

INT. CHAPEL - STAGE - DAY

Osiris looks at the screen.

                         OSIRIS
              What is this? Turn this off!

Kareem does not allow Osiris to move.

The men of The Hill are in hysterics.

Evers laughs uncontrollably.

Adam smiles uncomfortably.

ON SCREEN / INSERT

Osiris stares emotionless.

>   OSIRIS
>   Sunday, Bloody Sunday.

Maggie tosses aside the photo album. Turns to face Osiris.

>   MAGGIE
>   I love you.

>   OSIRIS
>   I love you, too.

INT. CHAPEL - DAY

The crowd is unsavory.

>   EVERS
>   Boo!

Oops. It catches on.

Osiris attempts to speak into the microphone.

>   OSIRIS
>   I can explain this-

Kareem sticks his hand over the microphone.

The crowd is unruly and tosses random TRASH on the stage.

Evers marches onto stage with his bible. He commandeers the
microphone.

>   EVERS
>   Wait a minute. Calm down. I have a
>   scripture I would like to read.

People continue to boo.

Evers flips to a page in his BIBLE. He speaks over the crowd.

                         EVERS
          What is done in the dark, shall come to
          the <u>White</u>.
                    (loses composure)
          Oops, I meant light.

MAYHEM.

Osiris bangs his staff twice on the floor.

                         OSIRIS
                    (shouts)
          Disciples, who am I?

Kareem raises his hand.

The Disciples of ANKH snap to attention.

Kareem locks eyes with Osiris. Kareem points to the side of the
stage.

The Disciples pivot right and march off stage.

Kareem snatches Osiris' staff and breaks it over his leg, tosses
it at Osiris, then exits the stage with the marching disciples.

Osiris removes his RING from his pocket. Stares at it.

INT. CHAPEL - OFF STAGE - DAY

Dean Richards observes from the side of the stage. He locks eyes
with Evers. They nod. Dean Richards lights a cigar, takes a drag,
then flicks ashes onto the stage.

                                             CUT TO:

EXT. CHAPEL - NIGHT

The lone STATUE of Frederick E. Hillfield, CHAINS draping from its
neck, towers in front of the baron walk of Hillfield Chapel.

                                             CUT TO:

INT. ANDERSON HALL - MEETING ROOM - NIGHT

Kareem addresses the Disciples of ANKH. They stand before him at
attention in a straight line.

                              KAREEM
                    Osiris set us back a few steps. We may
                    have lost a battle, but we will win the
                    war.

                    By any means necessary, we must elect
                    me, Kareem, the 1992 - 1993 Hillfield
                    University Student Government
                    President. We - shall - over - come!!!

Kareem holds up a fist with a single black glove.

                              KAREEM
                    Disciples, what is my name?

                             DISCIPLES
                    Sir, your name is Kareem, sir.
                         (roars)
                    Ra of ANKH, sir.

                              KAREEM
                    Victory! Victory!

All of the Disciples raise their right hands, which are covered with
BLACK LEATHER GLOVES.

                             DISCIPLES
                    Victory!!!

                                                    CUT TO:

INT. CLASSROOM - DAY

A classroom full of freshmen gaze glossy eyed at Dr. Mfume as she
meanders through the aisles of desks. The faint sound of random
SNORING emanates from an unknown location in the room. Winston and
T.J. sit near the back of the room.

                           DR. MFUME
                    It's a myth that the slaves could not
                    communicate with each other. They spoke
                    Portuguese and other languages that
                    they acquired while trading with
                    foreign countries. It was not uncommon
                    for Afrikans to be headmasters in
                    European schools because of this fact.

Adam sleeps and snores sitting up straight at the back of the room next to Liesl. A long string of DROOL slinks down from his lower lip to his desk. Dr. Mfume plants herself in front of Adam.

> DR. MFUME
> Next week, The Middle Passage. Class dismissed.

Students jump from their seats and press towards the door. Liesl attempts to wake Adam, but Dr. Mfume stops Liesl. The classroom empties leaving only Dr. Mfume and a catatonic Adam.

> SUDDENLY:

Adam awakens. He is startled to see an empty classroom and Dr. Mfume's eyes glaring at him.

> DR. MFUME
> My office.

> CUT TO:

INT. DR. MFUME'S OFFICE - DAY

Dr. Mfume sits behind her desk. Her office is decorated with AFRIKAN ART. Adam slouches in a hard chair before her desk.

> DR. MFUME
> (motherly)
> What's really going on, Adam?

> ADAM
> It's not what I thought it would be.

> DR. MFUME
> School?

> ADAM
> Life. It's not black or white. It's blurry.

> DR. MFUME
> Does the _end_ justify the means?

> ADAM
> Do the _means_ justify the end?

A beat.

Dr. Mfume looks out of her window.

CUT TO:

EXT. HUMANITIES BUILDING - DAY

Liesl waits along the side of the building. Adam slowly mopes out of the front door. Liesl catches him by surprise.

> LIESL
> You had something to do with what happened to Osiris today, didn't you.

Adam looks down.

> LIESL
> You really need to quit playing before somebody gets hurt or even killed.

Adam only stares at Liesl.

> LIESL
> Who gave you the right?

> ADAM
> I know what I'm doing. Trust   me. Once I'm a part of the system, I can change things.

> LIESL
> You don't get it, do you? You already are a part of the system and you haven't changed a damn thing for the better. You've only made them worse.

Adam affectionately touches Liesl on the shoulder.

> ADAM
> Let's get something to eat.

> LIESL
> No, I don't think so.

Liesl leaves Adam standing alone.

DISSOLVE TO:

INT. LIBRARY - DAY

Adam sits at a table as he flips through BOOKS.

INSERT

King James Bible - Matthew Chapter 26

                                        DISSOLVE TO:

INT. BLACK ROOM - DAY

Adam #1 sits at a table in the middle of the frame as he flips through
pages in a pile of books. Adam #2 walks to a dark stage.

A SPOTLIGHT illuminates stage number 1, located in the lower left
hand corner of the frame.

Osiris removes a GREEK DRAMA MASK FOR SORROW, kneels on the stage,
and holds his hands over his face.

                         ADAM (V.O.)
              Matthew, Chapter 26, Verse 75. And
              Peter remembered the word of Jesus,
              which said unto him, before the
              cockcrow, thou shalt deny me thrice.
              And he went out, and wept bitterly.

The lights go down on the stage.

                                        CUT TO:

BLACK SCREEN

An HOURGLASS on the left side of the screen drains WHITE sand from
the top of the hourglass to the bottom. The bottom is broken and
sand leaks out onto the bottom of the screen.

A HAND scoops white sand onto a pile of white sand on a SCALE. On
the other end of the scale is a stack of MONEY. As the extra scoop
of sand makes the sand side of the scale heavier and drop lower than
the money side, a word appears on the base of the sand side of the
scale:

                         MORALITY

                                        CUT TO:

INT. BOXING RING - NIGHT

Evers, dressed in a CLERGY COLLAR with a BIBLE clasp under his arm,
faces Hosea who wears an identical outfit. They both wear BOXING
GLOVES. The floor of the ring is covered with a FLAT MAP OF THE WORLD.

Adam stands in the center of the ring. He wears a LETTERMAN SWEATER, which reads: "THE HILL." He stares directly at the camera.

Chancellor Dix and Dean Richards sit ringside at the judges' table. They are respectively garbed in a GENERAL'S AND ADMIRAL'S MILITARY DRESS.

Liesl, dressed as a ring card girl, walks into the center of the ring. She holds up a RING CARD, which reveals the words:

(PREACHER -VS. - PREACHER)

Adam smacks the gloves of Evers and Hosea.

As Evers socks Hosea in the face, a BELL RINGS.

CUT TO:

INT. BLACK ROOM - DAY

A long cord extends from one end of the frame to the next. A tray of water for developing photos is at the bottom of the frame. We see a WHITE FLASH and hear a CAMERA SNAP PICTURES.

A NEGATIVE appears with THREE BLACK AND WHITE SHOTS of Hosea as he addresses a crowd in Chapel and the men of The Hill cheer him on. Morgan and Evers each hold up one of Hosea's hands high above his head.

The negative DISAPPEARS. Hands remove a PHOTO of one of the stills from the tray of water and hangs it on the cord with CLOTHES PINS.

ADAM (V.O.)

> Hosea gears up for his bid for the
> Student Government Presidency, but
> he's short on funds. Hosea has a good
> family name, but he does not come from
> money.

We see a WHITE FLASH and hear a CAMERA SNAP PICTURES.

A NEGATIVE appears with THREE BLACK AND WHITE SHOTS of Hosea as he walks across the Quad with TWO GIRLS in his arms.

The negative DISAPPEARS. Hands remove a PHOTO of one of the stills from the tray of water and hangs it on the cord with CLOTHES PINS.

> ADAM (V.O.)
> Hosea had traded his way to the top of
> the preachers by pimping Springfield
> sisters out to the less than desirable
> preachers.

We see a WHITE FLASH and hear a CAMERA SNAP PICTURES.

A NEGATIVE appears with THREE BLACK AND WHITE SHOTS of three Chapel
Assistants who shake hands with Hosea.

The negative DISAPPEARS. Hands remove a PHOTO of one of the stills
from the tray of water and hangs it on the cord with CLOTHES PINS.

> ADAM (V.O.)
> It wasn't long before he became popular
> and their leader. However, they don't
> know he's broke, an atheist, and not
> worthy in their eyes of the crown The
> Hill places before you.

ALL THREE PHOTOS move from left to right along the cord and out of
the frame.

We see a WHITE FLASH and hear a CAMERA SNAP PICTURES.

A NEGATIVE appears with THREE BLACK AND WHITE SHOTS where Hosea
removes a BROWN PAPER BAG from the trunk of a car and shakes hands
with Ronald Rollins.

The negative DISAPPEARS. Hands remove a PHOTO of one of the stills
from the tray of water and hangs it on the cord with CLOTHES PINS.

> ADAM (V.O.)
> Desperate to become King of The Hill,
> Hosea goes into business with Ronald
> Rollins, the Resident Director from
> Packard Hall, and secretly dope deals
> from his dorm room.

We see a WHITE FLASH and hear a CAMERA SNAP PICTURES.

A NEGATIVE appears with THREE BLACK AND WHITE SHOTS of a SPRINGFIELD
SISTER who throws a POT OF STEAMING COFFEE on Hosea.

The negative DISAPPEARS. Hands remove a PHOTO of one of the stills
from the tray of water and hangs it on the cord with CLOTHES PINS.

                              ADAM (V.O.)
                    After pissing off one of the mares in
                    his Springfield stable, the fallen
                    angel bids Evers for justice and
                    spreads Hosea's "tea."

We see a WHITE FLASH and hear a CAMERA SNAP PICTURES.

A NEGATIVE appears with THREE BLACK AND WHITE SHOTS where Evers
waves a BIBLE at Hosea. Hosea points aggressively at Evers.

The negative DISAPPEARS. Hands remove a PHOTO of one of the stills
from the tray of water and hangs it on the cord with CLOTHES PINS.

                              ADAM (V.O.)
                    Evers demands that Hosea step down as
                    Chancellor of the Chapel Assistants,
                    but Hosea refuses, and threatens Evers.
                    Evers does not hesitate to return the
                    favor.

                                                    CUT TO:

INT. CHAPEL - DAY

The Chapel Assistants are seated in the first few rows of the Chapel.
Hosea stands on the floor as he leans against the stage and addresses
the Chapel Assistants.

                              HOSEA
                    This hill sits right on top of the very
                    backs of the people who need us most.
                    We must to take back leadership of The
                    Hill.

                    And when we elect me, Hosea Johnson, the
                    1992 - 1993 Hillfield University
                    Student Government President, we shall
                    bringeth forth good fruit in the
                    vineyard.

APPLAUSE.

Evers taps Adam on the shoulder.

                              EVERS
                         (whispers)
                    Meet me in my room in an hour.

The Hill

A sea of encouraging Chapel Assistants surrounds Hosea. He catches
a glimpse of Evers who whispers to Adam.

                                                CUT TO:

INT. EVERS' DORM ROOM - NIGHT

Evers kneels at his bed deep in prayer as he clutches a CRUCIFIX.
His BIBLE is spread open before him on the bed. He breathes heavy.
BEADS OF SWEAT pummel down his face. There are KNOCKS at the door,
but Evers does not answer. More KNOCKS. Still he does not budge.
KNOCKS.

                          ADAM (O.S.)
                Evers, open the door. It's me, Adam.
                     (KNOCKS)
                I know you're in there. I can hear you
                breathing.
                     (JIGGLES DOOR KNOB)
                What's wrong? Open the door.

Evers slowly unlocks and opens the door. He retreats to his desk.
He pulls out a bottle of SCOTCH and TWO TUMBLERS from the back of
the bottom desk drawer.

                          EVERS
                Close the door.

Adam shuts the door and takes a seat on the bed.

                          ADAM
                Have you been drinking?

Evers pours a portion of scotch into both tumblers. Hands a glass
to Adam.

                          EVERS
                Drink. You're going to need it after you
                hear what I have to tell you.

Adam obliges.

                          EVERS
                There's no easy way to break this to
                you, so I'm just going to have to come
                right out and say it. It's Hosea, he's
                gone mad.

                          ADAM
                Mad?

                              EVERS
            He's selling drugs. Selling drugs right
            here on campus. Selling them right out
            of his dorm room.

                              ADAM
            It's a lie.

                              EVERS
            I didn't want to believe it either, but
            I confronted him and he admitted it. He
            even showed me his stash. It's hidden
            in the air vent above his desk.

            I asked him how a man of the cloth could
            do this, but he misinterpreted
            scriptures for his own purposes
            claiming the good of the few must be
            sacrificed for the good of the many.

            He's using the money he makes dope
            dealing to fund his campaign for the
            Student Government Presidency.

                              ADAM
            He's lost his mind.

                              EVERS
            If this gets out, not only will it
            damage the reputation of the Chapel
            Assistants, but the character of this
            institution, and the sanctity of
            Christianity. I don't think he even
            believes in God.

Evers grabs the bottle of scotch and swigs straight from the bottle.

Adam grabs the bottle.

                              ADAM
            Stop, that's not helping.

                              EVERS
            I'm so afraid. I don't know what to do.

A beat.

                    ADAM
Did you say that he keeps his stash in
the air vent above his desk?

                    EVERS
               (innocent)
Yes. Why?

                    ADAM
Don't worry. I'm going to fix this.

                    EVERS
What are you planning on doing?

                    ADAM
Have you told anyone else?

                    EVERS
No.

                    ADAM
Let's keep this between ourselves. For
now. Trust me.

Adam downs his scotch and leaves the room.

Evers takes a seat on the bed. Kicks off his shoes. He is relaxed.
Reaches behind the bed and grabs a spray bottle. Douses himself -
voilà, the beads of sweat.

Evers removes a cigar from his pocket and pops it into his mouth.
Evers whips out a pack of matches, which reads: "DEBRA'S". Evers
flips open the matches and inside the flap there is a phone number
written and the name: "TERRELL".

Evers lights the cigar and takes a deep drag. Mmm, good. He sprinkles
ashes, which fall, slowly onto his open Bible. Smiles.

                                        CUT TO:

INT. HOSEA'S DORM ROOM - DAY

An ALARM CLOCK RINGS. A HAND smashes the clock and CEASES TO RING.
Hosea hops out of bed. He's nude. Slips into a TERRY CLOTH BATH ROBE.
Slides into a pair of sandals. Grabs a huge TOILETRIES CASE. Leaves
the room.

                                        THEN:

Adam slips into the room. Grabs a chair. An IRON THUDS onto the floor. He freezes. No one enters. He positions the chair beneath the air vent. Searches. Nothing. Searches. Nothing. Searches. Got something. TWO POUNDS OF MARIJUANA and SEVERAL EMPTY DIME & NICKEL BAGS. The DIAMOND on Adam's GOLD PINKY RING with the initials "A.L.E." engraved on it SPARKLES.

INT. SHOWER - DAY

Hosea turns off the shower water. Steps out of the shower and towel dries himself off.

INT. HOSEA'S DORM ROOM - DAY

Adam quickly fills several dime bags. Pushes the stash back in its original hiding place. Moves the chair to the opposite side of the room. Opens another air vent in the ceiling. Stashes the dime bags that he's filled up.

We hear someone FUMBLING WITH THE DOOR KNOB.

EXT. HOSEA'S DORM ROOM - DAY

A hand turns the DOOR KNOB.

INT. HOSEA'S DORM ROOM - DAY

Adam hides in the closet. His eyes can be seen through a crack in the closet doors.

Claude Dubose (yeah, that fancy brother) sneaks into Hosea's room. Looks around. Searches Hosea's desk. Finds his wallet. Steals a CREDIT CARD. Slips back out of the room.

INT. MEN'S BATHROOM - DAY

Hosea brushes his teeth. Packs his toiletries case. Leaves the bathroom.

INT. HOSEA'S DORM ROOM - DAY

Adam slips out of the closet. Rushes out of the door.

                                        REVERSE TO:

INT. PACKARD HALL - HALLWAY - DAY

Adam quietly closes the door to Hosea's room. As he walks away from the door, he bumps into Hosea as he turns the corner.

                    HOSEA
          Adam, what are you doing in Packard Hall
          this time of morning?

                    ADAM
          My showers out. Gotta' run.

Adam pushes past Hosea.

A beat.

Hosea rushes into his room.

INT. HOSEA'S DORM ROOM - DAY

Hosea SLAMS his door and locks the top and bottom locks. He snatches
a chair and positions it under an air vent in the ceiling. Hosea
frantically removes the air vent. He reaches his hand into the
ceiling. A BEAD OF SWEAT oozes down Hosea's face. He slowly removes
his stash of MARIJUANA.

All there. A sigh of relief.

Hosea returns the marijuana to its hiding place and steps down from
the chair. He selects a PAIR OF SLACKS and a CLERGY COLLAR from his
closet and lays them across his bed.

INT. EVER'S DORM ROOM - DAY

Evers sits on his bed in boxers while Adam, high on adrenaline,
stands before him.

                    EVERS
          You want me to do what?

                    ADAM
          Call the Resident Director and have him
          search Evers' room.

                    EVERS
          Ronald Rollins is a preacher. What if
          he just tips off Hosea first about the
          search?

                    ADAM
          That's why I hid part of the stash in
          another air vent.

                   EVERS
               (maniacal)
       I can handle things from here.

                                 CUT TO:

INT. LAWRENCE'S DORM ROOM - DAY

Lawrence reclines on his bed as he reads a copy of SUN TZU'S THE
ART OF WAR. The PHONE RINGS. Eyes still focused on the book, his
hand reaches for the PHONE.

                 LAWRENCE
       Hello.

              DISGUISED VOICE (ON PHONE)
       If you want to get those damn preachers,
       now's your chance.

John Mason steps into the room. He wears a BATHROBE.

               JOHN MASON
       Who's that?

                         MATCH CUT TO:

INT. EVER'S DORM ROOM - DAY

Evers sits in his bed as he reads a copy of SUN TZU'S THE ART OF
WAR. A hand reaches for his nightstand to hang up the PHONE.

                                 CUT TO:

INT. MOTEL ROOM - DAY

Chancellor Dix sits with his back against the wall on his bed with
a copy of SUN TZU'S THE ART OF WAR. He wears a wig, make-up, and
a silk negligee. The PHONE on the nightstand RINGS. He reaches with
one hand for the phone.

              CHANCELLOR DIX
       Hello. I told you never to call me on
       this line unless it's. What? No,
       don't. I'm on my way.

                                 CUT TO:

EXT. PACKARD HALL - DAY

Chancellor Dix marches down the Quad with two white police officers
- OFFICERS SMITH AND WESSON. There are remnants of make-up on his
face. As Chancellor Dix reaches the steps of the dorm, Ronald
Rollins walks from around the back of the building. Ronald carries
TWO BAGS OF GROCERIES and wears a CLERGY COLLAR. He tries to stop
Chancellor Dix as Chancellor Dix storms toward the dorm.

                    RONALD
          Chancellor Dix, what's going on?

                    CHANCELLOR DIX
          I've got your boy Hosea.

Chancellor Dix pushes Ronald. His grocery bags tumble to the ground.
A JUG OF APPLE CIDER SHATTERS.

Ronald whips out a CELL PHONE.

INT. BATHROOM STALL - DAY

Hosea sits on the commode as he reads: "SUN TZU'S THE ART OF WAR".
He wears a CLERGY COLLAR. His pager goes off. He is startled. He
grabs it. It reads: "9-1-1."

                    HOSEA
          Shit!!!

INT. PACKARD HALL - STAIRWELL - DAY

Chancellor Dix and Officers Smith & Wesson march up the stairs.

INT. PACKARD HALL - HALLWAY - DAY

Hosea stumbles out of the bathroom with his pants still down around
his legs. He falls into the floor. Pulls his pants up. Rushes to
a GLASS CASE. Punches it. Pulls a FIRE ALARM.

Whips a BUTANE LIGHTER from his pants. Turns it to high. It ignites
a THREE FOOT FLAME. He holds it underneath a smoke detector. Sensors
light up. A CHEMICAL sand SPRAYS all over the building.

INT. PACKARD HALL - STAIRWELL - DAY

Chancellor Dix and Officers Smith & Wesson are bombarded by several
students who try to get out of the dorm. Chancellor Dix COUGHS on
the CLOUD OF DRY CHEMICAL EXTINGUISHER.

INT. BATHROOM STALL - DAY

Hosea flushes a last clump of MARIJUANA down the toilette.

INT. PACKARD HALL - HALLWAY - DAY

Hosea rushes back to his room. He bumps into Chancellor Dix and
Officers Smith & Wesson.

> HOSEA
> (innocent)
> I think I smell smoke.

Hosea stares at Chancellor Dix's face.

> HOSEA
> (perplexed)
> Is that make-up?

Chancellor Dix grabs Hosea by the ear.

> HOSEA
> Ow!

> CHANCELLOR DIX
> Come with me.

Chancellor Dix leads Hosea to his room.

Chancellor Dix kicks open Hosea's door. He looks at Officers Smith
& Wesson. Officers Smith and Wesson look at each other. Smith &
Wesson follow Chancellor Dix and Hosea into the room.

INT. HOSEA'S DORM ROOM - DAY

Chancellor Dix grabs a chair and goes directly to the air vent where
Adam hid the dime bags.

Hosea is puzzled.

Chancellor Dix removes the dime bags from the air vent.

> CHANCELLOR DIX
> (to Hosea)
> How do you explain this?

Chancellor Dix CHUCKS the dime bags at Hosea.

                              HOSEA
                        (truly sincere)
              Huh? It's not mine. I swear. It's not
              mine.

                          CHANCELLOR DIX
              Cuff him.

Police Officer smith removes HAND CUFFS from his utility belt.

                          OFFICER SMITH
              Place your hands on the wall and spread
              your legs.

                              HOSEA
              No, wait a minute.

                          OFFICER SMITH
              Place your hands on the wall <u>now</u>!

Hosea grabs Chancellor Dix by the arm.

                              HOSEA
              This is bullshit!

Officer Wesson grabs Hosea. Hosea pushes Officer Wesson off of him
and into the window hands first. The window SHATTERS and Officer
Wesson bloodies his hands.

                          OFFICER WESSON
              Fuck!

Officer smith swings his NIGHT STICK at Hosea. Hosea dodges the
swing and punches Officer smith in the face, which breaks Officer
Smith's nose. BLOOD spurts from Officer Smith's face.

                          OFFICER SMITH
              Aw, Christ!

Officer Wesson tackles Hosea and puts his knee into Hosea's neck.
Hosea struggles. Hosea claws at Officer Wesson's pants and tears
them.

                              HOSEA
              You're hurting my neck.

                          OFFICER WESSON
              Shut the fuck up!

Officer Smith puts his NIGHTSTICK around Hosea's neck. Hosea gags and urinates on himself.

Chancellor Dix taps Officer Smith on the back.

> OFFICER SMITH
> (pants)
> Stand back, sir!!!

> CHANCELLOR DIX
> (sincere)
> It's OK. Good job, Officers.

The Officers are stunned by Chancellor Dix's support of their actions.

> CUT TO:

EXT. THE QUAD - DAY

Hundreds of students are gathered in the Quad. They struggle to understand what's going on. Liesl is among them.

An AMBULANCE is parked on the grass in the center of the Quad.

Chancellor Dix and Officers Smith & Wesson exit the dorm accompanied by EMT GABRIEL and EMT MICHAEL who carry Hosea down the steps of the Dorm HANDCUFFED to a STRETCHER -lip busted, nose broken, blood smeared over his face, and a brace around his neck.

Adam looks at Hosea and is horrified. He then glances at Evers.

Evers holds up his hands as if to say he is just as surprised and appalled as Adam is.

Liesl spots Adam and makes her way in his direction.

EMT Gabriel and EMT Michael carry Hosea past Adam, Hosea goes into convulsions and spits up BLOOD. Hosea reaches with a free hand and grabs Adam by the hands.

> EMT GABRIEL
> Clear the fucking way!!!

EMT Gabriel and EMT Michael push students out of their way as they scurry towards the ambulance.

Adam looks at his HANDS. His hands and his GOLD PINKY RING engraved with the initials "A.L.E." are covered in BLOOD.

Lawrence LIGHTS a CIGAR. Slips it into his mouth.

As Hosea passes by, Lawrence takes a drag and puffs smoke into
Hosea's face. Lawrence sticks the cigar back into his mouth.

                                        MATCH CUT TO:

Evers removes a cigar from his mouth. As he watches the EMTs stuff
Hosea into the ambulance, Evers takes the cigar and breaks it in
half and lets both halves fall to the ground.

Liesl grabs Adam.

                    LIESL
            Please don't tell me you're a part of
            this, too?

Adam breaks down into Liesl's arm.

                    LIESL
            You're trembling.

TEARS stream down Adam's face. Adam looks Liesl in the eyes. Liesl
affectionately wipes away the tears.

                                        CUT TO:

INT. ADAM'S DORM ROOM - NIGHT

Liesl and Adam lie naked beneath the sheets in a post-coital
embrace.

                    LIESL
            Remember when you said if you got in too
            deep, you would get out?

                    ADAM
            Yes.

                    LIESL
            I think you're in too deep.

                    ADAM
            Are you asking me to become uninvolved
            in campus politics for you?

                    LIESL
            I'm asking you to become uninvolved for
            yourself.

                              ADAM
                    Tomorrow, after the Chapel Assistants
                    meeting, I'll tell Evers that I quit and
                    that I don't want anything else to do
                    with politics.

Liesl kisses Adam.

                                                    CUT TO:

INT. CHAPEL - DAY

The Chapel Assistants sit in the first few rows while Evers leans
against the stage as he addresses the Chapel Assistants.

                              EVERS
                    Yesterday's events were truly an
                    atrocity. I am convinced that it must
                    have been the Afrikans that set Hosea
                    up.

Nods of confirmation from the Chapel Assistants.

Morgan pounds his fist into the back of chair.

                              MORGAN
                    Goddamn Afrikans!

                              EVERS
                    None-the-less, the Chancellor has
                    called Hosea out and the damage is done.
                    Even once we clear his name; there will
                    always be doubt in the minds of the
                    student body.

                    True, time can heal the wounded heart,
                    but time is something that we don't have
                    a lot of here on The Hill.

                    I worked with Hosea very closely
                    formulating his community outreach
                    vision, and if we are the men we say we
                    are, it's our duty to see his vision
                    come to fruition.

                    That's why I will run for the 1992 - 1993
                    Hillfield Student Government
                    Presidency. And I will honor our fallen
                    brother's name.

APPLAUSE.

Evers is surrounded by supporting Chapel Assistants who pat him on the back.

Evers whispers into Adam's ear.

                    EVERS
          I want you to be my Chief of Staff.

Adam is silent.

                                        CUT TO:

INT. ADAM'S DORM - DAY

Adam dials a number of the PAYPHONE.

INT. LIESL'S DORM ROOM - DAY

Liesl sits at her desk writing in a notebook. The PHONE RINGS. She answers it.

                    LIESL
          Hello.

INTERCUT - ADAM AT PAYPHONE AND LIESL IN HER DORM ROOM

                    ADAM
          Guess who?

                    LIESL
          Hey, boo.

                    ADAM
          You're never going to believe this. The
          Preachers are supporting Evers as their
          Presidential candidate. Evers has
          asked me to be his Chief of Staff.
                    (beat)
          If we win, I could become the next
          Student Government President after
          Ever's term.

                    LIESL
          You're not just like all the others,
          you're worse. I really do hope you
          become Chief of Staff, President, or
          Emperor for all I care. I don't ever
          want to see you again. Vaya con dios.

Liesl hangs up the telephone.

                                              CUT TO:

INT. BATHROOM - DAY

Adam vociferously scrubs his hands under scolding steamy hot water
piping from the sink. He looks at his hands. They tremble. DRIED
BLOOD has stained his GOLD PINKY RING with the initials "A.L.E."
engraved on it. Adam turns his head away from the mirror. Adam scrubs
his hands more. Turns the hot water hotter. The palms of his hands
turn red. He scrubs them some more.

                                              CUT TO:

IN THE MIRROR

INT. LIBRARY - DAY

Adam sits at a table as he flips through BOOKS.

INSERT

King James Bible - Mark Chapter 8

                                          DISSOLVE TO:

INT. BLACK ROOM - DAY

There are three dark stages in triangle formation. Adam #1 sits at
a table in the middle of the frame as he flips through pages in a
pile of books. Adam #2 walks to the first stage.

A SPOTLIGHT illuminates stage #1, located in the lower left hand
corner of the frame.

Hosea stands on the backs of Homeless Henry and Kaneisha who lie
face down. Hosea removes a GREEK MASK FOR A HAPPY FACE. He is solemn.
Hosea holds a BUSHEL OF GOLD BRICKS in his arms.

                         ADAM (V.O.)
                MARK, Chapter 8, Verse 36. For what
                shall it profit a man, if he shall gain
                the whole world, and lose his own soul?

The lights go down on stage #1. Adam walks over to stage #2. It is
illuminated by a SPOTLIGHT.

Adam #1 opens another book.

The Hill

OVERLAY

1001 Things Everyone Should Know About Afrikan American History -
Part I Great Migration

John Mason & Terrell and Osiris & Kareem kneel at the front of the
stage with their hands tied behind their backs. Evers stands behind
them as he shakes hands with an Officer Smith.

                    ADAM
          It is a myth that most Afrikans who
          became slaves in America were captured
          by Europeans in slave raids. Most of the
          Afrikans who became slaves were sold
          into slavery by other Afrikans.

The LIGHTS GO DOWN on stage #2.

Adam #1 opens another book.

OVERLAY

A Hymnal - Amazing Grace

Adam #2 walks over to stage #3. It is illuminated by a SPOTLIGHT.

Officer Wesson lies across the backs of Pete, Morgan, and Jonas,
as he reads The Bible.

                    ADAM
          From 1619 - 1860, "The Good Ship Jesus"
          formerly the Mayflower, delivered over
          4 million Afrikans as slaves to the New
          World by Christians.

          John Newton was the captain of a slave
          ship, and it was on a slave ship where
          he penned the lyrics to Amazing Grace.

The LIGHTS GO DOWN on stage #3.

                                        CUT TO:

BLACK SCREEN

P.O.V. - INSIDE A CLOSET

INTENSE HEAVY BREATHING. The SOUND OF AN AX hacking at a closet door
echoes. With each strike, a PLANK OF WOOD BREAKS and an additional
ray of light streams into the closet.

The ax eventually becomes visible, as it is crashes through the closet door. The HANDS OF A SKELETON reach into the closet as it tears away the shards of wood until a full SKELETON is revealed, but immediately swallowed up by a WHITE LIGHT BURST.

A word appears on the screen:

PREFERENCES

CUT TO:

INT. BOXING RING - NIGHT

Evers and Terrell face Lawrence. Evers and Terrell wear both wear boxing gloves. The floor of the boxing ring is covered with a FLAT MAP OF THE WORLD.

Adam stands in the center of the ring. He wears a LETTERMAN SWEATER, which reads: "THE HILL." He stares directly at the camera.

Liesl walks into the center of the ring. She holds up a RING CARD, which reads:

(PREACHER - VS. - SUIT)

Adam taps Evers and Terrell on the gloves.

As Evers and Terrell both punch Lawrence, a BELL RINGS.

CUT TO:

INT. BLACK ROOM - NIGHT

In the frame, from left to right, are a LIGHT BOARD, an ASHTRAY with a SMOKING CIGAR, a MOVIE PROJECTOR, and a PROJECTOR SCREEN.

PROJECTOR SCREEN - CONTINUOUS

INT. HILLFIELD HALL - DAY

Students enter the building.

We hear a CAMERA SNAP A PICTURE. A PHOTO appears across the light board and the ashtray.

PHOTO

It's a still shot of the students who enter Hillfield Hall.

The photo reduces in size as it moves to the upper left-hand corner of the light board.

                         ADAM (V.O.)
              Whether or not there actually are
              "Toms" in Hillfield Hall, I can't tell
              you, but there definitely is treachery.

PROJECTOR SCREEN - CONTINUOUS

INT. CHANCELLOR DIX'S OFFICE - DAY

Chancellor Dix sits at his desk. Dean Richards barges into the
office as he angrily waves a SPREADSHEET.

                       DEAN RICHARDS
              Goddamn you, motherfucker!

We hear a CAMERA SNAP A PICTURE. A PHOTO appears across the light
board and the ashtray.

PHOTO

A still shot of Dean Richards as he angrily waves a spreadsheet
printout in Chancellor Dix's face.

The photo reduces in size as it moves to the light board.

                         ADAM (V.O.)
              For years something has been funny with
              the money, and now Dean Richards wants
              to up his cut...

                       CHANCELLOR DIX
              Fuck you!

                         ADAM (V.O.)
              But Chancellor Dix is through dealing
              with Richards' greed. Little does
              Chancellor Dix know, it's his own greed
              that he'll be through dealing with?

PROJECTOR SCREEN - CONTINUOUS

INT. DEAN RICHARD'S OFFICE - DAY

Dean Richards stands as he gazes out of his window. Evers enters
his office.

We hear a CAMERA SNAP A PICTURE. A PHOTO appears across the light
board and the ashtray.

PHOTO

A still shot of Lawrence who stands in front of Dean Richard's desk.

The photo reduces in size as it moves to the light board.

> ADAM (V.O.)
> Dean Richards summons his minions, and
> Evers is the first to respond to the
> dinner bell.

> EVERS
> You rang, sir?

> ADAM (V.O.)
> Do you want to be the 1992 - 1993
> Hillfield University Student
> Government President?

PROJECTOR SCREEN - CONTINUOUS

INT. CHANCELLOR DIX'S OFFICE - DAY

Evers enters Chancellor's Dix's office. Checks to see if anyone sees him enter. Closes the door behind him.

We hear a CAMERA SNAP A PICTURE. A PHOTO appears across the light board and the ashtray.

PHOTO

It's a still shot of Evers as he enters Chancellor Dix's office.

The photo reduces in size as it moves to the light board.

> ADAM (V.O.)
> Dean Richards arranges for Evers to
> work as a temporary assistant upstairs
> in Hillfield hall.

PROJECTOR SCREEN - CONTINUOUS

INT. CONFERENCE ROOM - DAY

Chancellor Dix addresses a room full of OLDER WHITE BUSINESSMEN dressed in suits and ties seated at a long table. Chancellor Dix is animated with his eyes wide and his lips protruding.

We hear a CAMERA SNAP A PICTURE. A PHOTO appears across the light board and the ashtray.

PHOTO

It's a still shot of Chancellor Dix as he addresses the businessmen.

The photo reduces in size as it moves to the light board.

>   ADAM (V.O.)
>   While Chancellor Dix is away on his
>   routine tour begging White
>   corporations for more money, for him to
>   steal.

>   CHANCELLOR DIX
>   After 400 years of enslavement, 10
>   years of Affirmative Action is not
>   enough to call it even.

PROJECTOR SCREEN - CONTINUOUS

INT. CHANCELLOR DIX'S OFFICE

Evers sits at Chancellor Dix's desk typing on the computer. Evers reaches into the bottom desk drawer and removes, a WIG, MAKE-UP, and PANTYHOSE.

We hear the SOUND OF A CAMERA TAKING A PICTURE. A PHOTO appears across the light board and the ashtray.

PHOTO

It's a still shot of Evers holding up the wig.

The photo reduces in size as it moves to the light board.

>   ADAM (V.O.)
>   Evers is able to uncover transactions
>   from Chancellor Dix's computer, which
>   reveal that he has been embezzling from
>   the Alumni Student Benevolent Fund by
>   making cash transfers to a dummy
>   corporation in Switzerland to pay for
>   a sex change operation.

>   EVERS
>   (smiles)
>   You're a bad, bad boy.

PROJECTOR SCREEN - CONTINUOUS

INT. CONFERENCE ROOM - DAY

Evers stands in a room as he addresses a group of SEVERAL MALE OLD
FOGIES who sit at a long pristine table

We hear a CAMERA SNAP A PICTURE. A PHOTO appears across the light
board and the ashtray.

PHOTO

It's a still shot of Evers as he addresses the Board of Trustees.

The photo reduces in size as it moves to the light board.

> ADAM (V.O.)
> Of course, Evers woefully shares this
> information with the Board of Trustees.

A single TEAR rolls down Evers' cheek.

> EVERS
> (melodramatic)
> I didn't want to come here.

PROJECTOR SCREEN - CONTINUOUS

EXT. HILLFIELD HALL - TELEVISION FRAME - DAY

Marsha Cohen stands in front of Hillfield Hall as she talks into
a microphone and to a TV CAMERA.

We hear a CAMERA SNAP A PICTURE. A PHOTO appears across the light
board and the ashtray.

PHOTO

It's a still shot of Marsha Cohen as she reports her story in front
of Hillfield Hall.

> ADAM (V.O.)
> Nor does Evers fail to notify that same
> pretty anchor woman from the Channel 6
> News who lambasted the Men of The Hill
> during the Afrikan take-over.

The Hill

                        MARSHA
Hillfield University Chancellor Dix
has just resigned under accusations of
embezzling from the University
Endowment Fund for a sex change
operation.

PROJECTOR SCREEN - CONTINUOUS

INT. CONFERENCE ROOM - DAY

Dean Richards stands at the head of the long table surrounded by
several old FOGIES who congratulate him.

We hear a CAMERA SNAP A PICTURE. A PHOTO appears across the light
board and the ashtray.

PHOTO

It's a still shot of the Trustees who congratulate Dean Richards.

                        ADAM (V.O.)
After Chancellor Dix resigns, lo and
behold, Dean Richards is named Acting
Chancellor of Hillfield University. To
the victor belong the spoils!

END PROJECTOR SCREEN

                                             CUT TO:

INT. ANDERSON HALL - HALLWAY - NIGHT

A POSTER, with a COLOR PHOTO of QUINCY COLLINS, who shakes hands
and poses with LAWRENCE JEFFRIES, hangs on the wall. It reads:

                        QUINCY COLLINS

                            ELECTS

                     LAWRENCE JEFFRIES

                        PRESIDENT

                         A <u>REAL</u> MAN!!!

     Paid for by The Committee to Elect Lawrence Jeffries.

A hand rips down the poster.

                                                          CUT TO:

INT. ANDERSON HALL - NIGHT

Two Disciples of ANKH, Disciple Malik and DISCIPLE GEORGE (20's),
stand guard in front of Kareem's door. T.J. approaches Kareem's
room. He attempts to knock on the door. They stop him.

INT. KAREEM'S DORM ROOM - NIGHT

Kareem sits in a WICKER BACK CHAIR as he clutches a LONG STAFF. His
room is filled with several disciples who type on computers, design
posters, write speeches, and review competitors' campaign
literature. Piles of left over wing specials and Styrofoam
containers clutter the room.

There's a KNOCK at the door. Disciple Jonas opens the door.

                         DISCIPLE GEORGE
                This brother has important information
                for Ra Kareem.

T.J. is allowed to enter the room. He stands before Kareem.

                              T.J.
                Kareem, sir, Ra of ANKH, sir. I bid you
                peace and blessings.

Kareem nods.

                              T.J.
                I have something that I reckon you
                should see.

T.J. reaches into his pocket. Disciples grab T.J.

Kareem holds up his hand and gestures that it's OK for T.J. to go
into his pocket.

T.J. removes the poster of Quincy and Lawrence. He hands it to
Kareem. Kareem examines it.

                            KAREEM
                Where did you get this?

                              T.J.
                This one came from Smith Hall, but
                they're all over the place. Lawrence's
                people just put them up.

The Hill

                    KAREEM
        Is there anything we can do for you?

                    T.J.
        My financial aid got fucked.

                    KAREEM
        We can fix that for you. There will be
        a place for you on the next line of ANKH
        should you wish.

                    T.J.
        I wish.

                    KAREEM
        Then, so shall it be. Peace and
        blessings unto you.

                    T.J.
        Peace and Blessings.

T.J. leaves the room. Jonas takes the poster from Kareem.

                    JONAS
        Goddamn it! Look at this bullshit.
        Fucking suits. They think they can get
        away with anything.

Kareem rises. He picks up a MAGAZINE.

                    KAREEM
        I'm about to take a shit. It's time for
        operation Chaka Zulu. I want you to
        contact every Disciple and every
        perspective Disciple of ANKH on this
        campus. And by the time I have wiped my
        ass, washed my hands, and walked back
        to this room
                (snatches poster from
                Jonas)
        I don't want there to be a single one
        of these Goddamn posters hanging
        anywhere.

Jonas steps back from Kareem.

                    JONAS
        Kareem, sir, Ra of ANKH, sir. It is
        already done, sir.

92.

                                        CUT TO:

SERIES OF SHOTS

INT. ANDERSON HALL - NIGHT

Various students simultaneously march out of their rooms.

INT. PACKARD HALL - NIGHT

Various students simultaneously march out of their rooms.

INT. SMITH HALL - NIGHT

Various students simultaneously march out of their rooms.

INT. ANDERSON HALL - NIGHT

Several posters of Quincy and Lawrence are torn from the walls.

INT. PACKARD HALL - NIGHT

Several posters of Quincy Lawrence are ripped to shreds and tossed
in the trash.

INT. SMITH HALL - NIGHT

"F.A.G." is spray painted over a single poster of Quincy and
Lawrence and set on fire.

END SERIES

                                        CUT TO:

EXT. DEBRA'S NIGHTCLUB - NIGHT

The marquee reads:

THE HILL NIGHT

INT. DEBRA'S NIGHTCLUB - NIGHT

Evers and Terrell sit at the bar as they sip on TUMBLERS OF SCOTCH.
Men of The Hill, who dance with each other, can be seen over Evers'
and Terrell's shoulders.

                    EVERS
          In return, I'll make you my Chief of
          Staff.

                         TERRELL
              I'll take it, but even without it, I
              would have done it anyway.

Evers smiles.

Terrell and Evers simultaneously whip out CIGARS. They both LIGHT
each other's cigar.

                                                  CUT TO:

EXT. CHAPEL - NIGHT

The marquee reads:

              STUDENT GOVERNMENT PRESIDENTIAL DEBATE

INT. CHAPEL - NIGHT

Evers, Lawrence, and Kareem sit at a long table on stage. Adam stands
at a podium positioned to the side of the stage.

APPLAUSE.

                         ADAM
              Thank you all, gentleman. This indeed
              has been a most exciting debate. May the
              best man win! Good night, everyone.

Adam connects EYES with EVERS, then leaves the podium. The
candidates leave the stage. People stagger, and converse, as they
prepare to leave the Chapel.

                                                  THEN:

Terrell walks from out of the audience onto the stage to the podium
and grabs the MICROPHONE.

                         TERRELL
              Attention my brothers! I need your
              attention please.

Lawrence is startled.

Kareem smiles.

                         KAREEM
              I have a funny feeling this is going to
              be good.

                         TERRELL
          As you know, I was going to run for
          Student Government President, but my
          former roommate, Lawrence Jeffries,
          had the minimum qualifying G.P.A.
          raised so that I might be ineligible.

Lawrence runs over to ADAM.

                         LAWRENCE
          What the hell is going on?

                         ADAM
          I don't know.

                         TERRELL
          I admit that I have a 2.9. And that is
          because instead of studying
          continuously, I devote a great portion
          of my time as a servant of the student
          body.

          Lawrence Jeffries would like you to
          believe that the stress and pressure of
          being Student Government President
          would be too great for me to handle in
          addition to my studies.

Lawrence grabs Adam.

                         LAWRENCE
          You're the Moderator. Do something. You
          have to stop him!

Lawrence shoves Adam.

                         ADAM
          He's a grown man, I can't stop him.

Evers sniffs a cigar.

                         LAWRENCE
          Somebody get security!
                    (turns to face Adam)
          Adam, you and your boy Evers are on my
          "X" list for life. Consider yourselves
          eternally damned.

                         TERRELL
          It is true that Lawrence Jeffries has
          a 3.7 GPA.

          But did you also know, that spring
          quarter, my freshmen year, Lawrence
          took an incomplete due to stress even
          though he was only taking one course.

          And why is that you ask. And so I will
          tell you.

Lawrence is horrified. He stands frozen.

Adam looks at Evers. Evers smiles.

                         TERRELL
          Lawrence was undergoing counseling and
          therapy because he could not deal with
          the fact that by day he was a heroic
          homosexual hater and by night he was
          flaming fag.

SILENCE!!!

                         TERRELL
          The male organ of The Hill is erect and
          Lawrence Jeffries is sucking it.

Terrell leaves the stage.

Chaos erupts in the Chapel.

Winston grabs Adam by the neck.

                         WINSTON
                       (astonished)
          Did you participate in this?

Adam doesn't say anything.

                         WINSTON
          You're a bastard.

Evers connects EYES with Lawrence. Evers moves his cigar in and out
of his mouth like a penis. Chuckles.

Lawrence remains frozen, and the chaos swarms around him.

                                             CUT TO:

INT. LAWRENCE'S DORM ROOM - NIGHT

Lawrence stands in front of his open window with the butt of a smoldering cigar in his hand.

A Special Bulletin News Broadcast plays on the:

TELEVISION

INT. NEWSROOM - NIGHT

Marsha Cohen sits at a news desk as she holds a stack of papers in front of her. In the upper left hand corner of the screen is a PICTURE of O.J. & NICOLE BROWN-SIMPSON.

> MARSHA
> We just got shocking news that Nicole
> Brown-Simpson, wife of football legend
> O.J. Simpson, has just been found
> stabbed to death in her Brentwood home.

END TELEVISION

As the GOLD EMBERS of the cigar reach Lawrence's fingertips, we hear the SINGE of the fire go out.

> CUT TO:

EXT. LAWRENCE'S DORM - NIGHT

Lawrence jumps out of his window.

INT. ADAM'S DORM ROOM - NIGHT

We hear a loud THUD as Adam is violently awakened from a deep sleep. Could this have been a nightmare?

> CUT TO:

Winston stands in the doorway with the door wide open.

> WINSTON
> I hope you fuckers have joy. Lawrence
> Jeffries is dead. He killed himself.

> CUT TO:

INT. BATHROOM - NIGHT

Adam scrubs his hands underneath scolding hot water. He looks at them. They tremble. Adam pours bleach on his hands and scrubs them some more.

                                                    CUT TO:

IN THE MIRROR

INT. BLACK ROOM - DAY

There are two dark stages in triangle formation. Adam #1 sits at a table in the middle of the frame as he flips through pages in a pile of books. Adam #2 walks to the first stage.

A SPOTLIGHT illuminates stage #1, located in the lower left hand corner of the frame.

Terrell and Lawrence face each other as they prepare to strike with OVERSIZED BOOMERANGS.

                         ADAM (V.O.)
               Exodus, Verse 21, Chapter 24. Eye for
               eye, tooth for tooth, hand for hand,
               foot for foot.

The lights go down on stage #1. Adam walks over to stage #2. It is illuminated by a SPOTLIGHT.

Adam #1 opens another book.

OVERLAY

1001 Things Everyone Should Know About Afrikan American History - Part I Great Migrations

Twelve students total stand in a straight line on the stage: Four Suits (Quincy Collins, John Mason, Pete, & Cleo), Four Preachers (Hosea, Evers, Morgan, & Ronald), and Four Afrikans (Osiris, Kareem, Jonas, & Dashon).

                         ADAM (V.O.)
               During World War II, there were 407,316
               American lives lost.

The Suits leave the stage.

                              ADAM (V.O.)
                    During the Civil War, there were
                    558,052 American lives lost.

The Preachers leave the stage.

                              ADAM (V.O.)
                    During the slave trade, there were
                    approximately 12 million people
                    transported from Afrika with the
                    intention of being slaves.

                    Only about 10 million made it to their
                    destination. The rest perished.

The Afrikans leave the stage.

The LIGHTS GO DOWN on stage #2.

                                                    CUT TO:

BLACK SCREEN

A ROARING FIRE burns across the bottom of the screen.

                         ...IN THE END

                                                    CUT TO:

BLACK SCREEN

SEVERAL RATS scurry through a MAZE towards a single piece of CHEESE
positioned in a RAT TRAP, which reads:

                         <u>CHAOS</u>

A single RAT reaches the cheese.

                                              CUT TO BLACK:

SNAP.

                                                    CUT TO:

BLACK SCREEN

All of the Pre-Alumni Members, Chapel Assistants, and Disciples of
ANKH are in the ring in an ALL OUT BRAWL.

Adam stands motionless in the center of the screen. He wears a LETTERMAN SWEATER, which reads: "THE HILL." He stares directly at the camera.

Acting Chancellor Richards sits ringside in an Admiral's military dress at the judges' table. Chancellor Dix is hunched over the table with a KNIFE stuck in his back. Police Officers storm the ring and join the brawl.

Liesl, dressed as a ring card girl, walks into the center of the ring as she carries a RING CARD. Officers Smith & Wesson violently grab Liesl and toss the ring card towards the camera. The Ring card travels and spins in slow motion to reveal these words as it moves directly in front of the camera:

(EVERY MAN 4 HIMSELF)

A BELL RINGS.

CUT TO:

The frame is split into two equal halves. The right half is divided into four equal quadrants - screens 1 - 4. The left half of the screen is one big screen - screen 5.

SCREEN 5

INT. ANDERSON HALL - DAY

A POSTER OF EVERS hangs on the wall. Next to the poster of Evers, is a larger poster of KAREEM.

ADAM (V.O.)
Decision 91 has come down to Evers,
Kareem, and Cleo Wallingford, the
Student Court Justice - a write in
candidate that the Pre-Alumni Members
decided to support.

HANDS HOLD A COLOR POSTER OF CLEO WALLINGFORD:

WRITE IN

Cleo Wallingford

PRESIDENT

Paid for by The Committee to Elect Cleo Wallingford.

100.

DARK HANDS set it on FIRE and drop it into a TRASH CAN full of other
Cleo Wallingford posters.

                                                    CUT TO:

INT. STUDENT COURTROOM - NIGHT

A group of students shake hands with Morgan. Evers taps Morgan on
the shoulder and whispers into his ear.

                         ADAM (V.O.)
                Luck is a residue of design. Evers makes
                a deal with Dean Richards and Morgan is
                magically named Elections Committee
                Chairman.

INT. ACTING CHANCELLOR RICHARD'S OFFICE - NIGHT

Acting Chancellor Richards sits behind his desk and flips open a
box of cigars.

                         ADAM (V.O.)
                The fix is in.

Evers and Morgan reach into the box of cigars. They light them and
take a puff. Smiles.

The previous action from SCREEN 5 moves to and continues on SCREEN
1.

SCREEN 5

INT. MEETING HALL - DAY

Students wait in line to vote. There is a long table with elections
committee members with stacks of PRINTOUTS. Morgan sits at the end
of the table. As a student stands before a committee member, the
student flashes his student ID.

A committee member hands a student a BALLOT and a PEN. The student
fills out the ballot, folds it in half, drops it into a wooden box,
and returns the pen. Dr. Mfume sits at another end of the table.
She collects all of the pens, and distributes a different set of
colored pens.

>   ADAM (V.O.)
>   The Hill is still quite antiquated and
>   only one or two percent of students
>   actually vote.
>
>   The deal is that Morgan will cross off
>   extra names when no one is watching to
>   the sum of 50 extra votes.

The previous action from SCREEN 5 moves to and continues on SCREEN 2.

SCREEN 5

INT. ADAM'S DORM ROOM - DAY

Evers, the most trusted Chapel Assistants, and other candidates in on the fix are huddled around the room as they rapidly fill out ballots. There's a knock at the door.

Adam opens the door without stopping to check to see who it is. Everyone in the room jumps and tries to hide the ballots. The person on the other side of the door turns out to be Morgan. He hands everyone a new set of colored pens.

>   ADAM (V.O.)
>   Morgan comes to my dorm room to let us
>   know what color to use. I look the most
>   innocent, so I'm drafted to make the
>   drop.

The previous action from SCREEN 5 moves to and continues on SCREEN 3.

SCREEN 5

INT. HILLFIELD HALL - MEETING ROOM - DAY

Adam suspiciously walks into the polling place. He wears an overcoat while everyone else wears TANK TOPS and SHORTS.

                              ADAM (V.O.)
               In the dead of summer, I go into the
               polling area wearing a grossly
               oversized Inspector Gadget style
               overcoat.

               The 50 extra ballots are in my outside
               coat pocket. When it's my turn to insert
               my ballot, I hold the 50 ballots in my
               coat sleeve.

               As I stick my hand on the ballot box,
               the sleeve slides down covering the
               slot in the box.
               Within the blink of an eye, I slyly
               stuff 50 extra ballots into the ballot
               box.

Dr. Mfume grabs Adam by the arm.

                              DR. MFUME
                         (congenial)
               Are you familiar with Dr. Frances
               Cress-Welsing and her "Theory of Color
               Confrontation"?

The action from SCREEN 5 moves to and continues on SCREEN 4.

SCREEN 5

INT. HILLFIELD HALL - SMALL MEETING ROOM - NIGHT

Adam celebrates. The others pout.

                              ADAM (V.O.)
               When Evers and our crew win the
               election, there are complaints.

PRE-ALUMNI PETE sticks his hand into the ballot box.

                              PRE-ALUMNI PETE
               All these ballots say the exact same
               thing for every office. The election
               has been fixed!

A Disciple of ANKH Poll Watcher looks at the TALLY SHEETS.

                    DISCIPLE DASHON
          The number of names crossed off on the
          sign-in sheet and the number of ballots
          cast is off by 5 votes.

                       DR. MFUME
          In the last 25 years of Hillfield
          University history, never before has
          the count been that close. It's usually
          off by 50 votes.

Adam looks at the camera.

                         ADAM
          Mission accomplished!

END SPLIT SCREENS

                                              CUT TO:

INT. ACTING CHANCELLOR RICHARDS' OFFICE - DAY

Terrell sits across from Acting Chancellor Richards at his desk.
Richards has his feet propped up on his desk and his nose buried
in SUN TZU'S THE ART OF WAR.

                  ACTING CHANCELLOR RICHARDS
                  (nose still in book)
          Elections at The Hill never seem to be
          without drama.
                  (looks up from book)
          Have you ever read this book? Sure you
          have. Great book. Today is your lucky
          day. I am greatly displeased with the
          results thus far of this year's Student
          Government Presidential Election.

                       TERRELL
                  (puzzled)
          Sir?

                  ACTING CHANCELLOR RICHARDS
          All loose ends must be eliminated. With
          or without the drama, life goes on.
          Should the drama continue, it will
          become necessary for the lambs to
          follow a temporary shepherd.

Acting Chancellor Richards looks around his new office.

Terrell smiles.

Richards opens the box of cigars on his desk.

                                        CUT TO:

EXT. ADAM'S DORM - ROOFTOP - DAY

Adam stands at the edge to take in a view of all of The Hill. Adam's
back is to Terrell, who is a few paces behind him.

                    TERRELL
          The Hill is a microcosm of the real
          world. Everything you experience here,
          you will experience in the world, but
          tenfold.

Adam continues to take in the view. Terrell steps next to Adam. Puts
his arm around Adam. Points Adam's head towards the ground. It's
a long way down.

                    TERRELL
          Evers is going down. Are you going with
          him? No, you're not. And why is that?
          Because you're going to knock him down.

                    ADAM
              (mumbles)
          No.

                    TERRELL
          What was that?

                    ADAM
              (mumbles)
          No.

                              TERRELL
          It's called C.Y.A. Adam. You're debt to
          Evers. You're a liability. You know too
          much.

          Those are the rules of the game. By any
          means necessary, if you don't take him
          down, he'll take you down.

          What? Did he offer you Chief of Staff?
          Well, Adam, he offered me Chief of
          Staff, too. Just as Evers must
          eliminate you, there are higher powers
          that must eliminate Evers.

          I'll be named Acting Student Government
          President and you'll be my Chief of
          Staff.

                              ADAM
                         (mumbles)
          No.

                              TERRELL
          Then who should run next year's Student
          Government, Adam? Evers? Is that
          what the people need? How many more
          bodies will he bury between now and the
          end of next school year? If you want
          to stand against something, stand
          against that.

                                                  CUT TO:

INT. LIESL'S DORM ROOM - DAY

CLAUDE DUBOSE is lip-locked with the figure of an unrecognizable
Springfield freshman sister. Claude tries to slide his hand up the
girl's shirt, but she stops him.

                              CLAUDE DUBOSE
                         (whispers)
          Come on.

                              LIESL
                         (moans)
          No.

The PHONE RINGS.

                        ADAM (O.S.)
                  (on answering machine)
            Liesl, I just wanted you to know that
            I've been thinking about what you said.

Liesl raise her head into view.

                        ADAM (O.S.)
                  (on answering machine)
            I already am a part of the system, but
            I haven't done anything to change it.
            I won't you to know I love you and I'm
            going to make things right.

Claude tries to unzip Liesl's pants, but she stops him.

                        LIESL
            No.

Claude goes for her pants again.

                        CLAUDE DUBOSE
            Come on!

Liesl twists Claude's arm behind his back.

                        LIESL
            No means no!

Liesl leads Claude to her door. She opens it.

                        CLAUDE DUBOSE
            Ow, fucking freshman!

Liesl kicks Claude in the rear, out her doorway, and slams the door
shut behind him.

                                        CUT TO:

INT. BATHROOM - DAY

Adam scrubs his hands in the sink. He turns up the hot water. Steam
fogs up the mirror.

                                        CUT TO:

IN THE MIRROR

INT. BLACK ROOM - NIGHT

John Mason, Hosea, and Osiris stare at an apple tree in the middle
of the stage. They point at the fruit and hesitate to take a piece.

>   ADAM (V.O.)
>   **Genesis, Chapter 2, Verses 16 & 17.** And
>   the LORD God commanded the man, saying,
>   of every tree of the garden thou mayest
>   freely eat:
>
>   But of the tree of the knowledge of good
>   and evil, thou shalt not eat of it: for
>   in the day that thou eatest thereof thou
>   shalt surely die.

END MIRROR

                                                   CUT TO:

INT. INTENSIVE CARE UNIT - DAY

Hosea lies on a hospital bed with an OXYGEN MASK on his face and
several TUBES that stick out of his arms. A HEART MONITOR BEEPS.

EXT. THE QUAD - DAY

Dr. Mfume slowly walks with a PAD under her arm towards an OLD FIRE
BELL.

INT. ANDERSON HALL - MEETING ROOM - DAY

Kareem and several Disciples form a long line. The perspective
disciples are huddled into a group. T.J. is among them. They all
have their hair twisted into sprouting baby dreadlocks.

>   KAREEM
>   Many were called, but few were chosen.
>   Who will be man enough to be the first
>   to walk down the line?
>
>   T.J.
>   I will Kareem, sir, Ra of ANKH, sir.
>
>   KAREEM
>   Then so be it.

EXT. THE QUAD - DAY

Osiris stands in the center of a mob of young men and women.

>   OSIRIS
>   They just arrested O.J. Simpson for the
>   murder of his wife. Free O.J.!!!

INT. ACTING CHANCELLOR RICHARDS OFFICE - DAY

Acting Chancellor Richards sits at the head of the table. Present
are Dr. Mfume and a couple of other faculty members in addition to
Evers, Adam, Terrell, Kareem, and Cleo Wallingford. Evers and Adam
sit at opposite sides of the table.

>   ACTING CHANCELLOR RICHARDS
>   In light of all the information that has
>   been presented...

INT. ANDERSON HALL - MEETING ROOM - DAY

T.J. steps in front of Malik. Malik punches T.J. in the chest. T.J.
gasps.

INT. ACTING CHANCELLOR RICHARDS' OFFICE - DAY

Cleo wipes sweat from his brow.

>   ACTING CHANCELLOR RICHARDS
>   It leaves me no choice, but to decree
>   the immediate expulsion of Evers...

INT. ANDERSON HALL - MEETING ROOM - DAY

T.J. steps in front of Dashon. Dashon punches T.J. in the chest.
T.J. breathes heavy.

INT. ACTING CHANCELLOR RICHARDS' OFFICE - DAY

Evers slams his hand on the table.

>   ACTING CHANCELLOR RICHARDS
>   And the temporary appointment of
>   Terrell as Acting Student Government
>   President...

INT. ANDERSON HALL - MEETING ROOM - DAY

T.J. steps in front of Jonas. Jonas punches T.J. in the chest. Beads
of sweat stream down T.J.'s face.

INT. ACTING CHANCELLOR RICHARDS' OFFICE - DAY

Adam holds his head down.

                    ACTING CHANCELLOR RICHARDS
          Until this matter can be further
          resolved.

INT. INTENSIVE CARE UNIT - DAY

Hosea twitches.

The STEADY BEEP BECOMES UNSTABLE.

EXT. THE QUAD - DAY

Dr. Mfume RINGS the old fire bell. Students gather around.

The HEART MONITOR BEEPS.

INT. ANDERSON HALL - MEETING ROOM - DAY

T.J. staggers to Kareem. Kareem punches T.J. in the chest. T.J.
collapses. He pants frantically.

The HEART MONITOR BEEPS.

EXT. STREET - DAY

Osiris leads a mob of marching students through the middle of the
street. He is in the middle of several male and female students who
hold a SPRAY PAINTED SHEET, which reads:

                    FREE O.J.

Traffic is backed up on all side streets.

                    ALL STUDENTS
                      (chants)
          FREE O.J. FREE O.J. FREE O.J.

Homeless Henry climbs out of a TRASH DUMPSTER and joins the
marchers.

                    HOMELESS HENRY
          Free O.J.

The HEART MONITOR BEEPS.

INT. ACTING CHANCELLOR RICHARDS OFFICE - DAY

Terrell smiles.

> CLEO
> This is bullshit.

> KAREEM
> Can he do that?

> EVERS
> Motherfucker.

The HEART MONITOR BEEPS.

INT. INTENSIVE CARE UNIT - DAY

Hosea goes into convulsions.

The UNSTABLE BEEPS BECOME A LONG CONTINUOUS TONE.

EXT. THE QUAD

The heart monitor TONE CONTINUES.

Dr. Mfume no longer rings the bell. She is surrounded by several
Chapel Assistants, Pre-Alumni members, and Disciples of ANKH.

> DR. MFUME
> The election has been thrown out.
> Terrell has been appointed Acting
> Student Government President until a
> new election can take place.

EXT. THE QUAD - DAY

The heart monitor TONE CONTINUES.

Morgan is surrounded by a mob of male and female students.

> MORGAN
> Hosea is dead! The Afrikans killed
> him. Fuck the Afrikans!!!

INT. ANDERSON HALL - MEETING ROOM - DAY

The heart monitor TONE CONTINUES.

PERSPECTIVE DISCIPLE JIMMY runs over to T.J. and tears open T.J.'s
shirt.

                         fiJIMMY
             Give him some air. He's gone into
             cardiac arrest.

EXT. STREET - DAY

The heart monitor TONE CONTINUES.

A row of all AFRIKAN-AMERICAN Policemen in RIOT GEAR with and
SHOTGUNS and RUBBER BULLETS march towards the peacefully
demonstrating students.

A car on a side street rear-ends another car. There is a crash. A
Policeman fires into the crowd. Lavette (T.J.'s honey) gets hit in
the EYE by a rubber bullet.

INT. ACTING CHANCELLOR RICHARDS' OFFICE - DAY

The heart monitor TONE CONTINUES.

Evers pushes over the conference table onto Adam. He leaps over the
table and tries to strike Adam, but the other guys pull him off.

                    ACTING CHANCELLOR RICHARDS
             Security!!!

INT. INTENSIVE CARE UNIT - DAY

Hosea lies motionless in his hospital bed.

The LONG CONTINUOUS TONE continues. No one enters the room.

EXT. THE QUAD - DAY

The heart monitor TONE CONTINUES.

Chapel Assistants, Pre-Alumni members, and Disciples of ANKH
complain.

                    DISCIPLE DASHON
             What?

                    CHAPEL ASSISTANT CHAD
             Come on!

INT. ANDERSON HALL - MEETING ROOM - DAY

Jimmy administers CPR to T.J. - breathing life into his mouth and
pounding hope onto his chest.

The heart monitor TONE CEASES.

EXT. STREET - DAY

An Officer gets hit in the neck by a bottle. Screams. The crowd disperses. Dogs are released on the crowd. The Policemen chase after them.

INT. TERRELL'S DORM ROOM - DAY

Terrell looks out of his window down at the Quad.

                                        SUDDENLY:

His door is SMASHED open. It's...

                    TERRELL
          John Mason?

John points a HANDGUN at Terrell.

                    JOHN MASON
          Mother Fucker. I trusted you. It wasn't
          enough to kill my future, but you had
          to kill my lover, too.

                    TERRELL
          You mean Lawrence. Wait a minute. You
          got it all wrong.

John Mason empties an entire clip into Terrell's chest. Terrell crashes through the window and falls to the ground.

EXT. THE QUAD - DAY

A WORLD WAR II AIR-RAID SIREN RINGS CONTINUOUSLY. The Policemen and dogs chase the students through the campus. It's utter chaos. A dog chews on a guy's ankle. Students try to get into the dorms, but they are shot or clubbed. Tear gas is launched into the center of the Quad. Liesl is among them.

EMT Gabriel and EMT Michael try to push through the crowd while they carry T.J. on a stretcher. An OXYGEN MASK covers T.J.'s face.

Adam stands frozen on the steps of his dorm as he watches the chaos. Liesl is shot with a rubber bullet in front of him. Liesl falls on the steps.

                    ADAM
              (softly)
      No.
              (normal tone)
      No.
              (screams)
      Nooooooooooooooooooooooooo!!!
      Nooooooooooooooooooooooooo!!!
      Nooooooooooooooooooooooooo!!!

Officer Black tries to strike Liesl with a BATON. Adam leaps from
the steps and grabs the baton and punches the Officer Black, which
knocks Black down to the ground.

Officer Wesson tries to strike Adam from behind in the head with
a baton, but a Chapel Assistant, adorned in a clergy collar, tackles
Smith.

Students overturn the AMBULANCE.

Officer Wesson is tossed head first through the first floor window
of a dormitory.

Anderson Hall is set on FIRE.

Students from each dorm turn FIRE HOSES onto the Police.

                                                      CUT TO:

The morning after...

EXT. HILLFIELD HALL - DAY

GROUNDS MEN remove the words:

                    NO JUSTICE. NO PEACE.

Spray-painted across the front doors of the Hillfield Hall.

INT. ACTING CHANCELLOR RICHARDS' OFFICE - DAY

Adam stands across from Acting Chancellor Richards on the other side
of Acting Chancellor Richards' desk. They shake hands.

                    ACTING CHANCELLOR RICHARDS
              I'm appointing you acting Student
              Government President.
              Congratulations, Adam. You'll be
              Hillfield University's first Sophomore
              Student Government President.

Acting Chancellor Richards reaches into a cigar box. His HAND TWITCHES. He removes TWO CIGARS from a box. He LIGHTS both of them.

Adam walks over to the window. Peers through the glass and surveys the previous day's aftermath.

EXT. THE QUAD - DAY

Windows are broken. HAZE and MIDST rises from the ground. Cars are over-turned. BLOOD is stained on the pavement.

EXT. CHAPEL - DAY

A lone STATUE of Frederick E. Hillfield, BLOOD smeared on it's face, towers in front of the BLOOD-STAINED, TRASH strewn walk of Hillfield Chapel.

INT. ACTING CHANCELLOR RICHARDS' OFFICE - DAY

Acting Chancellor Richards steps away from his desk. Stands next to Adam.

                    ACTING CHANCELLOR RICHARDS
          I was a Hillfield Student Government
          President, too.
                    (beat)
          Look how far we've come.

Acting Chancellor Richards hands Adam a cigar. The DIAMOND ON Adam's GOLD PINKY RING engraved with the initials "A.L.E." sparkles for a moment from a single ray of sunlight squeezing through the window.

Adam's hand twitches. He takes a drag. Coughs profusely. He takes another drag. Coughs a little less. Takes another drag. Coughs even less. Takes another drag. Holds it in. Blows smoke out of his nose.

                                        CUT TO:

INT. CABIN - NIGHT

A WOODEN PLAQUE is tossed into a FLAMING FIREPLACE amidst the ashes of the burning SKETCHES from the opening of the film.

THE HILL MAIN THEME slowly rises.

WOODEN PLAQUE

Hillfield University

Proudly presents this plaque to

Acting Student Government President

1995 - 1996

Adam Lawrence Evers

SUPERIMPOSE SERIES OF SHOTS

INT. STUDENT COURTROOM - DAY

A SHORTHAIRED, GOATEED ADAM, wearing a JUDGE'S ROBE, SLAMS a gavel. Adam wears his DIAMOND GOLD PINKY RING with the initials "A.L.E." engraved on it.

EXT. GRAVEYARD - NIGHT

A SHORTHAIRED, GOATEED ADAM wearing a SWEAT SUIT holds a CROWN above his head while the morning sunrise shines through it. Adam wears his DIAMOND GOLD PINKY RING with the initials "A.L.E." engraved on it.

INT. CHAPEL - NIGHT

A BALDHEADED, CLEAN-CUT ADAM adorned in a CLERGY COLLAR holds a LANTERN to his face while he preaches from the makeshift pulpit. Adam wears his DIAMOND GOLD PINKY RING with the initials "A.L.E." engraved on it.

EXT. HILLFIELD HALL - DAY

A BALDHEADED, CLEAN-CUT ADAM adorned in a CLERGY COLLAR stands CHAINED to the doors with a MEGAPHONE IN HIS HAND. Adam wears his DIAMOND GOLD PINKY RING with the initials "A.L.E." engraved on it.

INT. MAGGIE'S DORM ROOM - NIGHT

A DREDLOCKED ADAM lies on a twin bed engaged in a long passionate embrace and kiss with MAGGIE. Adam wears his DIAMOND GOLD PINKY RING with the initials "A.L.E." engraved on it.

INT. DEBRA'S NIGHTCLUB - NIGHT

A SHORTHAIRED, GOATEED ADAM sits at the bar sipping on a tumbler of SCOTCH and writing on the inside flap of a BOOK OF MATCHES.

116.

INT. ADAM'S DORM ROOM - NIGHT

A BALDHEADED, CLEAN-CUT ADAM adorned in a clergy collar gives a BAG
OF MARIJUANA to a pair of HANDS. The hands hand Adam a WAD OF MONEY.
Adam wears his DIAMOND GOLD PINKY RING with the initials "A.L.E."
engraved on it.

INT. ANDERSON HALL - MEETING ROOM - NIGHT

A DREDLOCKED ADAM punches a YOUNG DISCIPLE OF ANKH in the chest.
Adam wears his DIAMOND GOLD PINKY RING with the initials "A.L.E."
engraved on it.

INT. CHANCELLOR DIX'S OFFICE - DAY

A SHORTHAIRED, GOATEED ADAM removes a WIG from Chancellor Dix's
DESK. Adam wears his DIAMOND GOLD PINKY RING with the initials
"A.L.E." engraved on it.

INT. DEAN RICHARD'S OFFICE - NIGHT

A BALDHEADED, CLEAN-CUT ADAM adorned in a CLERGY COLLAR, smokes
CIGARS with Dean Richards. Adam wears his DIAMOND GOLD PINKY RING
with the initials "A.L.E." engraved on it.

INT. SMITH HALL - NIGHT

A HAND points a PISTOL at a DREDLOCKED ADAM'S FACE while Adam stands
in front of a window. Adam attempts to grab the gun. Adam wears his
DIAMOND GOLD PINKY RING with the initials "A.L.E." engraved on it.

INT. ANDERSON HALL - NIGHT

A PAIR OF HANDS tear down a COLOR POSTER of a DREDLOCKED ADAM, which, reads:

ELECT

ADAM LAWRENCE EVERS

PRESIDENT

Paid For By The Committee To Elect "A.L.E."

The hands toss the poster into a FLAMING GARBAGE CAN.

END SERIES

INT. CABIN - NIGHT

The plaque slowly burns until it is black with ash and encompassed in flames.

FADE OUT:

FINIT.